RIGHTS & RESPONSIBILITIES
·of Doctors·

The British Medical Association

Rights and Responsibilities of Doctors

A publication from the BMA Professional Division.

Project Director:	Dr John Dawson
Project Editor:	David Morgan
Consultant Editors:	Charles Butcher
	Anne Stanesby
Editorial Secretariat:	Audrey Porter
	Julie Stone
	Hilary Curtis
	Hilary Glanville
	Stan Jenkins
Graphic Designer:	Glynn Bennallick

© **British Medical Association 1988**
First Printed July 1988

British Library Cataloguing in Publication Data:
British Medical Association (Professional Division).

RIGHTS AND RESPONSIBILITIES OF DOCTORS

ISBN 0 7279 0236 9

Published by: British Medical Association, Tavistock Square, London WC1H 9JP

Printed by: Burgess & Son (Abingdon) Ltd, Oxon. Typeset by: Megaron, Cardiff. In association with Godfrey Lang.

Contents

1

2

3

4

5

6

7

8

9

10

Glossary

A action – the formal legal demand of one's rights from another person brought in court; a lawsuit.

ambit – the compass of actions, words, etc.

appeal – the process by which a decision of a lower court is brought for review before a court of higher jurisdiction. The party bringing the appeal is the appellant. The party against which the appeal is taken is the appellee.

assault – both crime and civil wrong. Any examination involving touching the body, investigation or operation without consent constitutes an assault.

B **bona fide** – in good faith; genuinely.

breach – the breaking of any legal or moral bond or obligation; violation, infraction.

C **cadaver** – a corpse; a lifeless human body used for dissection.

canvassing – soliciting votes, orders, contributions, etc.

civil (courts) – pertaining to the private rights and remedies of a citizen; as distinguished from criminal, political, etc.

claimant – one who makes or enters a claim; one who has a claim upon anything.

Class A drug – see controlled drugs.

clinical trial – defined in Section 31(1) of the Medicines Act 1968 as: 'an investigation or series of investigations consisting of the administration of one or more medicinal products of a particular description:

a   by, or under the direction of, a doctor or dentist to one or more patients of his, or

b   by, or under the direction of, two or more doctors or dentists, each product being administered by, or under the direction of, one or other of those doctors or dentists to one or more patients of his,

where (in any such case) there is evidence that medicinal products of that description have effects which may be beneficial to the patient or patients in question and the administration of the product or products is for the purpose of ascertaining whether, or to what extent, the product has, or the products have, those or any other effects, whether beneficial or harmful.'

common law – the part of Anglo-American law that is derived from court decisions rather than from statutes and regulations. In England, the ancient customary law of the land.

confidentiality – the principle of maintaining the security of information elicited from an individual in the privileged circumstances of a professional relationship.

The individual has a fundamental right to privacy; and this is of particular importance in the practice of medicine when the unauthorised disclosure of personal information may have personal, social or legal repercussions. On the other hand, information about him of a medical nature may have to be released to fulfil a statutory obligation such as the completion of a certificate of the causes of death, a document legally open to inspection by the public. The patient himself may release the doctor from the bond of secrecy by asking him in writing to report on his clinical condition to an employer, insurance company or solicitor.

congenital disabilities – disabilities existing before birth or at birth; dating from birth.

consent – consent to medical or surgical treatment obtained by implication (implied), word of mouth (verbal) or, on paper, signed (written), necessary to avoid subsequent allegation of operative or other procedure without approval.

contempt (of court) – scorn, disgrace; in law, disregard of the rule, or an offence against the dignity of a court.

contract – a legally enforceable agreement between two parties in which each agrees to do something.

controlled drugs – substances which are controlled drugs are listed in Schedule 2 of the Misuse of Drugs Act 1971 and the degree of legal control depends to some extent on which 'class' the substance is in. Drugs considered to be most socially damaging when misused are listed in Part 1, Class A Drugs. Stringent restrictions are placed on those who may possess, supply, import or export controlled drugs. Section 2(2) of the Act permits amendment of the classes and new additions and removals occur from time to time.

Examples of drugs listed in Schedule 2:

Class A includes: alfentanil, cocaine, dextromoramide, diamorphine (heroin), dipipanone, lysergide (LSD), methadone, morphine, opium, pethidine, phencyclidine, and class B substances when prepared for injection.

Class B includes: oral amphetamines, barbiturates, cannabis resin, codeine, ethylmorphine, glutethimide, pentazocine, phenmetrazine, and pholcodine.

Class C includes: certain drugs related to the amphetamines such as benzphetamine and chlorphentermine, diethylpropion, mazindol, meprobamate, methyprylone, pipadrol, and most benzodiazepines.

coroner – a judicial officer whose duty is to enquire into the manner of death of any person who is suspected of dying an unnatural death, or of one for which the cause is not evident, also of all persons dying in prison, and all deaths among persons certified as suffering from mental disease. Such deaths include those due to violence and industrial disease, and as a result of anaesthetics, and deaths among persons in receipt of disability pensions. He is appointed by the local authority and must be possessed of a legal or medical qualification and have practised for at least five years.

crime – a violation of law, especially if serious: an act punishable by law.

Crown immunity – immunity from prosecution granted by the Crown.

D **damages** – the value estimated in money of something lost or withheld; the sum claimed or awarded in compensation for loss or injury sustained.

defendant – a person sued in a court of law; the party in a suit who defends.

disclaimer – a denial, disavowal, or renunciation.

disparage (ment) – to dishonour by comparison with what is inferior; to match in marriage with an inferior, to lower in rank or estimation; to talk slightingly of, to dishearten.

due care – the legal duty one owes to another according to the circumstances of a particular case. It is that care which an ordinarily prudent person would have exercised in the given situation; the absence of negligence.

E **enact** – to make into an act; hence, to ordain, decree.

enactment – the action of enacting (a law); the state of being enacted.

equitable – 1. Characterised by equity or fairness. 2. Pertaining to the department of jurisprudence called EQUITY; valid in equity as distinct from law.

ethics – the science of moral conduct. Medical ethics: the moral rules and principles which govern a member of the medical profession in the exercise of his profession.

ex parte – on behalf of, on the application of, one party; by or for one party. An ex parte judicial proceeding is one brought for the benefit of one party only without notice to or challenge by an adverse party.

executor – one who executes or carries out; an agent, doer: a person appointed by a testator to execute or give effect to his will after his decease.

exemption – immunity from a liability, obligation, penalty, law or authority; freedom.

exonerate – to free from (a duty, obligation, payment, charge, etc; also, from blame).

F **fraud** – criminal deception; the using of false representations to obtain an unjust advantage or to injure the rights or interests of another.

G **goodwill** – established popularity of a business, treated as a saleable asset.

I **in toto** – entirely.

informed consent – a doctrine that states that before a patient is asked to consent to a risky or invasive diagnostic or treatment procedure he is entitled to receive certain information: (a) a description of the procedure; (b) any alternatives to it and their risks; (c) the risks of death or serious bodily disability from the procedure; (d) the probable results of the procedure, including any problems of recuperation and time of recuperation anticipated; and (e) anything else that is generally disclosed to patients asked to consent to the procedure.

inquest – a legal or judicial enquiry to ascertain or decide a matter of fact, especially one made by a jury in a civil or criminal case. Formerly, a general term for all formal or official inquiries.

inquiry/enquiry – the action of seeking especially (now always) for truth, knowledge, or information concerning something.

inter alia – amongst other things.

J

Jehovah's Witnesses – the International Bible Students Association.

K

kin (next of) – the person (or persons) standing nearest in blood relationship to another, and entitled to share in his personal estate in case of intestacy.

L

legislation – the action of making or giving laws: the enactment of laws, law-giving.

liability – the condition of being liable or answerable by law or equity.

liable – bound or obliged by law or equity; answerable (for, also to); legally subject or amenable to.

licentiate – one who has obtained a licence to exercise some function; eg one who has received a formal attestation of professional competence or of proficiency in some art from some collegiate or other examining body.

litigation – the action of carrying on a suit in law or equity; legal proceedings.

loco parentis – doctrine which permits a court to appoint a person to stand in the place of parents and assume all of their legal rights, duties, and obligations with respect to a child.

locum tenens – a medical practitioner who acts as deputy for another.

M

maladministration – inefficient or improper management of affairs especially public affairs.

manslaughter – criminal homicide without malice aforethought.

medical referee – a doctor attached to the Cremation Authority who must have not less than five years' standing and relevant experience and qualifications.

medicinal – 1. Having curative or healing properties. 2. Belonging to or of the nature of a medicine.

medicinal product – Section 130 of the Medicines Act 1968 defines what is meant by a medicinal product as follows:

The definition includes 'any substance or article (not being an instrument, apparatus or appliance) which is manufactured, sold, supplied, imported or exported for use wholly or mainly in either or both of the following ways, that is to say:

a   use by being administered to one or more human beings or animals for a medicinal purpose;

b   use, in circumstances to which this paragraph applies, as an ingredient in the preparation of a substance or article which is to be administered to one or more human beings or animals for a medicinal purpose.

Later it is stated that this paragraph applies to '(a) use in a pharmacy or in a hospital; (b) use by a practitioner; (c) use in the course of a business which consists of or includes the retail sale, or the supply in circumstances corresponding to retail sale, of herbal remedies.'

Various items are exempt from the definition medicinal product, the most relevant being bandages and other surgical dressings (except medicated dressings where the medication has a curative function which is not limited to sterilising the dressing).

medicinal purpose – is defined as any one or more of the following purposes:

a   treating or preventing disease;

b   diagnosing disease or ascertaining the existence, degree of extent of the physiological condition;

c   contraception;

d   induction anaesthesia;

e   otherwise preventing or interfering with the normal operation of a physiological function, whether permanently or temporarily and whether by way of terminating, reducing or postponing, or increasing or accelerating, the operation of that function or in any other way.

minors – under age; below the age of majority (18 years).

misprision – a wrongful action or omission; a misdemeanour or neglect of duty on the part of a public official.

N

negligent – inattentive to what ought to be done; neglectful; indifferent of actions or conduct.

notifiable disease – designated infectious disease, the occurrence of which must by law be reported to health authorities.

O

ombudsman – (Health Service Commissioner) empowered by Statute to investigate complaints from people who claim that they have sustained injustice or hardship as a result of an alleged failure of a regional or area health authority to provide a service which it was a function of that body to provide, or as a result of an alleged failure in a service provided by such a body, or as a result of maladministration in the provision of a service by such a body.

order – the rule of law or proper authority.

P

patent – a conditional and limited monopoly granted by the State as a reward for the introduction into the realm of new technology. Inventions in the medical field patentable under British law include new drugs per se, processes for making drugs, synergistic combinations of drugs, and surgical appliances.

plaintiff – the person who brings a lawsuit against another.

post mortem – after death examination of a body, including its organs, in order to establish the cause of death.

precognition – awareness of an event before it has happened, sometimes taking the form of a detailed vision of the event.

Privy Council – a private consultation or assembly for consultation. The private counsellors of the sovereign.

procurator fiscal – in Scotland, the public prosecutor of a shire or other local district.

project licence – granted by the Secretary of State to specify a programme of work and authorise the application as part of that programme of specified places.

product liability – under Part I of the Consumer Protection Act 1987, producers of defective products are strictly liable.

proviso – 1. A clause inserted into a legal or formal document making some condition, stipulation, exception or limitation. 2. Or upon the observance of which the operation or validity of the instrument depends.

pupils – girls under the age of 12 and boys under the age of 14.

Q **quasi (proprietal)** – as if, as it were. In composition, in a certain manner, sense, or degree: in appearance only.

R **regulations** – rules promulgated by an administrative agency, following specified procedures (eg public notice and public hearings), under the authority of a statute.

remand – to send back for further proceedings, as when a higher court sends a case back to a lower court.

repealed – 1. To revoke, annul (a resolution, a law, sentence, etc). 2. To recall, withdraw (a privilege, grant, etc). 3. To withdraw or retract a statement.

restrictive covenant – a formal agreement, contract which restricts the setting up of competitive business.

S **standing** (must not have less than five years') – 1. To be or remain valid or of force; to remain good. 2. To be or remain in a specified condition, relation, situation, etc.

statute – 1. A law or decree made by a sovereign or legislative authority. 2. An enactment containing one or more legislative provisions, made by a legislature of a country at one time, and expressed in a formal document; the document in which such an enactment is expressed.

statutory duty – a moral and legal obligation enacted, appointed or created by statute; conformable to the provisions of a statute.

statutory instrument – statutory: enacted by statute; depending on statute for its authority. Instrument: a writing containing a contract; a formal record.

stillbirth – the lifeless state of birth. Failure to breathe or show any other sign of a separate existence upon expulsion from the body of the mother. Term commonly used only for gestations of 28 weeks or more (prior to this, referred to as products of abortion).

subpoena – a court order compelling a witness to appear and testify in a certain proceeding.

sue – 1. To institute a suit for, make a legal claim to; hence to petition or appeal for; to seek to obtain. 2. To institute legal proceedings against (a person): to prosecute in a court of law; to bring a civil action against.

summons – 1. An authoritative call to attend at a specified place for a specified purpose. 2. A call or citation by authority to appear before a court or judicial officer.

T **third party** – other person/s; not self.

tort – 1. Injury, wrong. 2. The breach of a duty imposed by law, whereby some person acquires a right of action for damages.

treason – 1. The action of betraying. 2. Violation by a subject of his allegiance to his sovereign or his state.

tribunal – a court of justice; a judicial assembly; place of judgement or decision.

U **ultimus haeres** – in law, the Crown or the State, which succeeds to the property of those who die intestate, or without next of kin.

V **vested** – not contingent or suspended, hence (law) already acquired.

vicarious liability – filling the place of another: exercised, performed or suffered by one person or thing instead of another.

vis à vis – opposite number.

W **ward of court** – someone (usually a child) under the protection of a court.

warrant – a writ for arresting a person or for carrying a judgement into execution.

witness – one who sees or has personal knowledge of a thing: one who gives evidence.

Index

Table of Cases

Table of Circulars and Notices

Table of Statutes

Table of Statutory Instruments

Books and Reports

Banks MAL. (Chairman) **British patent system; report of the committee to examine the patent system.** (Cmnd. 4407). *London, HMSO, 1970*

British Medical Association. **Deaths in the community.** *London, BMA, 1986.*

British Medical Association. **The handbook of medical ethics.** *London, BMA, 1986.*

British Medical Association. **The torture report.** *London, BMA, 1986.*

Clerk JF and Lindsell WHB. **Clerk and Lindsell on torts.** 15th ed. *London, Sweet and Maxwell, 1982.*

Criminal Law Revision Committee, **11th Report, Evidence – General.** (Cmnd 4991). *London: HMSO, 1972.*

Department of Health and Social Security. **Cadaveric organs for transplantation. A code of practice, including the diagnosis of brain death, drawn up and revised by a working party on behalf of the Health Department of Great Britain and Northern Ireland.** *London: HMSO, 1983.*

Ellis N. **Employing Staff,** 2nd ed. *London: BMJ, 1987.*

General Medical Council. **Professional conduct and discipline: fitness to practise.** *London, GMC, 1987.*

General Medical Services Committee. **Guidance to general medical practitioners on data protection registration.** *London: BMA, 1988.*

General Medical Services Committee. **Guidance to general medical practitioners on the subject access provisions of the Data Protection Act.** *London: BMA, 1987.*

Halsbury's laws of England. 4th ed. *London: Butterworths, 1973–85.*

Law Commission. **Breach of confidence.** (Cmnd 8388). *London: HMSO, 1981.*

Law Reform Committee, **16th Report Privilege in Civil Proceedings** (Cmnd 3472). *London: HMSO 1967.*

MacLennon H. (Chairman). **Advice from the Advisory group on transplantation problems on the question of amending the Human Tissue Act 1961.** (Cmnd 4106). *London: HMSO, 1969.*

Mason JK and McCall Smith RA. **Law and medical ethics.** 2nd ed. *London: Butterworths, 1987.*

Painter AA. ed. **Butterworths law of food and drugs.** *London: Butterworths, 1981.*

Rogers WVH. ed. **Winfield and Jolowicz on tort.** 12th ed. *London: Sweet and Maxwell, 1984.*

Introduction

The rights and responsibilities of doctors have developed in parallel with the medical practitioner's ability to intervene to identify, and cure or alleviate disease. For example, scientific advances in the understanding of infectious organisms have been accompanied by a series of Public Health Acts made by Parliament during the 19th and 20th centuries. Many of the powers and duties laid down in these Acts are beyond the scope of the individual – for instance supervision of housing, control of sewage, drainage and water supplies, inspection of foodstuffs – but others impose specific obligations on registered medical practitioners. Thus a number of diseases must by law be notified to the proper officer of the local authority by the doctor in charge of the case.

In these and many other matters, registered medical practitioners have rights and responsibilities, duties and powers which require them to do, or not to do, certain things in certain circumstances.

The British Medical Association (BMA) is a voluntary association set up in 1832 'To promote the medical and allied sciences, and to maintain the honour and interests of the medical profession'. The BMA is the professional association of doctors in the United Kingdom and advises doctors both collectively and individually on the professional and ethical aspects of their work and actions in relation to their patients, their colleagues and society as a whole. It receives a constant stream of enquiries about all non-clinical aspects of medical practice. Many are dealt with on the spot but some require painstaking research and consultation with lawyers or other specialists.

The report *Rights and Responsibilities of Doctors* was intended originally as an internal document, a collection of information which could be used to provide advice to members of the Association and to which could be added the results of research performed in response to future enquiries. However, as the project developed it was recognised that many doctors, medical students, and others such as health service administrators, lawyers with interests in medical practice, and local authority officers, would welcome a handbook which could be used directly. This first edition is being published now so that those interested can have access to the results of work done so far while the Association continues to research other areas. The Secretary of the Association would welcome suggestions for further entries that can be researched and included in a subsequent edition.

1

What this book is and what it is not

The aim of this book is to provide a practical guide to certain aspects of the law as it affects doctors. It is not, of course, possible to deal with everything. It is hoped though that the book will cover the main areas that most doctors would wish to know about. As the BMA receives numerous queries about the law it is possible to have some idea of the questions most often asked. The law is continually changing and any doctor with a specific problem should check that no amendment has occurred following the publication of this report.

Every person has a duty to behave lawfully and the sanctions for not doing so can be considerable. If a criminal offence has been committed the offender can be prosecuted in the criminal courts where a penalty such as a fine or, in serious cases, a sentence of imprisonment could be imposed. Other breaches of the law could result in a civil law suit and an award of damages against the wrongdoer.

Doctors have additional codes of conduct to observe. The General Medical Council (GMC) has a statutory power to suspend or erase the registration, if they think fit, of any registered medical practitioner who is found by their Professional Conduct Committee 'to have been convicted in the British Islands of a criminal offence' or who is judged by that committee 'to have been guilty of serious professional misconduct'. Doctors working in the National Health Service (NHS) can be referred to the GMC as a result of investigation by a Service Committee of allegations of breaches of terms and conditions of service.This book is not intended to be a comprehensive guide to the sorts of misconduct which could lead to disciplinary proceedings and readers should refer to the GMC current guide *Professional Conduct and Discipline: Fitness to Practise* (1987) referred to as the 'blue booklet'.

The doctor also has the issue of medical ethics to consider. Sometimes the law may conflict with what the doctor sees as his ethical duty. This book is not intended to be a guide to medical ethics and readers should refer to the BMA *Handbook of Medical Ethics* for further guidance on this subject.

How to use this book

The book has ten chapters each containing a number of sub-topics linked to the main heading. The issue of confidentiality, for instance, is first discussed in general and then considered particularly in relation to, for example, the difficulties doctors may face when confronted with a patient who they suspect has committed a serious crime or who has a disease which must by law be notified to an outside authority.

The topics covered are listed in the contents pages, but if the subject you wish to know about does not seem to be there then turn to the index at the beginning of the book, which we have tried to make as comprehensive as possible. It is likely that the topic that you are interested in is in fact referred to in one of the chapters. For instance, AIDS is not a notifiable disease, but certain provisions in the Public Health (Infectious Diseases) Regulations 1985 (S.I. 1985 No 434) do apply. The law relating to AIDS is therefore detailed in the chapter relating to notifiable disease, although there is not sufficient space to indicate that fact in the contents list at the beginning of the book.

A brief guide to law

Some people who use this book will have extensive knowledge of the law but others will not and it is for the benefit of the latter that the following explanations are made.

The sources of law in England and Wales are, firstly, legislation and secondly, decided court cases. Sometimes a situation crops up which is not covered by any existing statute nor by any decided court case. The reader will find several instances of such legal vacuums whilst consulting this book. When this occurs all a lawyer can do is to look at the other authorities which are not law but which may well influence a judge's decision. Examples of such are the opinions of academic lawyers as expressed in recognised law text books, decisions made in law courts in other countries and, of particular relevance in the field of medical law, circulars emanating from official bodies such as the Department of Health and Social Security (DHSS). To assist those readers who know very little about our legal system, further explanation is given in the next three paragraphs about the process of legislation and the role of decided court cases.

At various times throughout this book we shall be referring to Acts or Statutes (both words mean the same thing). Acts of Parliament are primary legislation and become law after they have been passed by both Houses of Parliament and have received the Royal Assent. An Act may come into force immediately or at a later date, or it may be introduced in stages. This can make life very difficult for the writers of guides to the law. They may know that there is a new statute waiting in the wings to be brought into operation whereas at the time of writing the old law still applies. When we have set out the law as it will be in the future rather than as it is at present we have of course made that clear, and readers who are members should refer to the BMA for guidance as to the current state of the law if they need advice concerning it.

We shall also be referring the reader to numerous Statutory Instruments. These are usually known as Regulations or Orders and are sometimes called 'delegated legislation' because when an Act has been passed by Parliament to deal with a particular situation, Parliament can, at the same time and in the body of the Act, delegate to the Secretary of State the right to draw up Regulations to deal with details or future situations which it is not possible or appropriate to include in the main Act. The Statutory Instruments Act 1946 provides for various procedures by which a Statutory Instrument can come into force and become law. There is not space here to explain fully these procedures which are very complicated. Briefly the Statutory Instrument must either:

1   Be laid before Parliament before it comes into operation (which means Parliament must legislate to revoke it), or

2   Be laid before Parliament with forty days' time limit being given within which objections can be made, or

3   Be laid before Parliament in draft and approved by resolution.

Regulations have the force of law but they can only be drawn up if there is an Act of Parliament already in existence from which the right to make the particular Regulation derives.

Decisions made in the English courts are an important source of law. Blackstone defined the common law as 'the ancient unwritten law of this kingdom'. Common law is the law of the land embodied in judicial decisions as opposed to statutory law or law enacted by Parliament. Court decisions may be the only authority concerning a particular issue or they may be the authority which decides how a particular piece of legislation is to be interpreted, as it is not possible to legislate for every situation that might occur. Legislation can be passed to change the rule of law in a decided court case and to that extent court cases are subordinate to the rule of Parliament. Courts must follow decisions made by courts superior in the hierarchy. To avoid a complete stalemate, however, the House of Lords can in certain circumstances decide not to follow a decision that it made previously.

Scotland: The law in Scotland differs fundamentally from that in England and Wales. Different statutes apply, and the system of courts and legal officers is different; for example in Scotland there are procurators fiscal, *some* of whose powers and duties are similar to those of English coroners. In a volume of this size, it is not possible to describe all the relevant differences between Scottish and English law, but some representative examples are mentioned. Thus this book should be used only for general guidance in Scotland; people requiring definitive information are strongly advised to consult a Scottish lawyer or the Scottish Office of the BMA.

Europe: The entry into the European Economic Community in 1972 has necessitated changes in UK law to effect harmonisation between its member states. Regulations approved by the Council of Ministers become UK law as soon as they are passed. EEC Directives require enabling UK legislation to be passed within a certain time.

4

1 Consent

1.1 Consent to Treatment

It is generally unlawful for a doctor to treat a patient without first obtaining the latter's consent to the treatment in question. If a doctor were to treat a patient against the latter's wishes, the doctor could find himself at risk of an action for assault or negligence.

Obviously where an operation, for example, is involved it is highly desirable to obtain the patient's written consent where possible.

There have been a number of court cases concerning the issue of what is sometimes called 'informed consent'. Patients who have suffered injury as a result of receiving medical treatment have attempted to sue the surgeon for negligence on the basis that they were not given adequate information about the risks involved in the treatment, the argument being that had they been fully informed they would never have agreed to have the treatment in question. The legal position at the moment can be summed up best as follows.

A surgeon does have a duty to warn the patient of risks inherent in the procedure so that the patient can make an informed decision as to whether or not to consent. However, if the surgeon warns of the risks which a recognised body of medical opinion considers the patient ought to be warned of then the patient probably will not succeed in any action for medical negligence (see Chapter 6, Medical Negligence, where the case of Bolam v Friern Barnet HMC [1957] 2 AER 118 is discussed because the principle laid down in that case has been applied to the issue of informed consent).

Example: Sidaway v Bethlem Royal Hospital [1985] 1 AER 643. A patient became paralysed following an operation upon her cervical vertebrae. The operation carried a small risk of damage (about 2%) to the nerve root or spinal cord. Damage to the cord would produce a far more serious result and the risk of that happening was less than 1%. The surgeon warned of the risk of damage to the nerve root but not of the risk to the spinal cord. The eventual decision of the court was that the patient could not succeed in her claim for damages for negligence for failing to warn of the risk of damage to the spinal cord. The surgeon was acting in accordance with recognised medical practice. (See also the case of Freeman v the Home Office [1984] 1 AER 1036 CA discussed in subchapter 5.2.4, Consent to Treatment.)

1.2   Jehovah's Witnesses

Jehovah's Witnesses present a special problem for doctors in that they will not permit any form of tissue transplantation, a policy most commonly manifested by their refusal to accept blood transfusions. It is necessary to distinguish between adult and child Jehovah's Witnesses as the doctor's responsibility differs according to their status.

1.2.1   Adult Jehovah's Witnesses

If an adult Jehovah's Witness refuses to consent to a blood transfusion then legally that treatment cannot be given. Even if the Jehovah's Witness were mentally confused there still is no procedure for imposing treatment on someone who has refused consent (subchapter 1.1, Consent to Treatment).

If a Jehovah's Witness is suffering from a condition, the normal treatment for which may involve a blood transfusion, then the BMA *Handbook of Medical Ethics* (paras 10.15–10.16) gives guidance as to what a doctor should do in the event of the Jehovah's Witness refusing to consent to a transfusion being given. We suggest that if the doctor decides to continue the treatment despite the risk which the refusal gives rise to then the patient should be warned of the extent of this risk. It is advisable to give such a warning in the presence of a witness. If despite the warning the patient still will not agree to recommended procedures being taken then he should be asked to sign a written acknowledgement to that effect and to the effect that he understands what increased risks will result from such refusal.

1.2.2   Children of Jehovah's Witnesses

If a child's parents will not consent to necessary medical treatment this could place the doctor in a difficult position. In England and Wales the Family Law Reform Act 1969, Section 8(10) provides that a person who has attained the age of 16 may validly consent to surgical, medical and dental treatment and such consent is to have the same effect as if the person was of full age. In Scotland the Children and Young Persons (Scotland) Act 1937, Section 12, contains similar provisions. This means that if a young person who was aged 16 or over agreed to have treatment then the parents could not override the young person's decision whatever their religious views.

The position regarding children under 16 is regulated by the common law, there being no relevant statute. It is considered advisable when treating such children to first obtain the consent of the parent or guardian. There is support though for the view that if a young person has the necessary understanding of what is involved then any consent by him to medical treatment would be valid despite parental objection. (See the case of Gillick v West Norfolk and Wisbech AHA and the DHSS [1985] 3 WLR 830 3 AER 402, discussed in subchapter 2.4, Disclosure to the Family and Non-relatives.)

In Scotland there are two categories of young persons in the eyes of the law:

minors and pupils. Minors are young people under the age of 18 and pupils are girls under the age of 12 and boys under the age of 14. It is likely that the Scottish courts would take the view that there was a presumption that a minor would be capable of understanding the procedures involved and possible consequences and hence of giving valid consent and that a pupil would not be so capable.

What is the situation where a child will not or is too young to give informed consent? It is possible that court proceedings could be commenced so that the treatment in question could be legally sanctioned on behalf of the child. In England and Wales this could be achieved by making the child a ward of court and then obtaining the necessary permission from a High Court judge. In Scotland, local authorities have powers under the Social Work (Scotland) Act 1968 (as amended) to take children into care and in prescribed circumstances to assume parental rights by authority of the court, but these procedures take time.

However, National Health Service Circular No. 1975 (GEN)81 states that to take such court proceedings is an inappropriate course. Instead the following advice is offered: 'The decision whether or not to provide a blood transfusion or to operate to save the life of a child, despite the wishes of the child's parents, should be taken by the consultant concerned on the basis of his clinical judgement and after a full discussion with the parents. A consultant would run little risk in a court of law if, in acting according to his conscience, he obtained:

(a) the written supporting opinion of a medical colleague that the patient's life was in danger if the treatment were withheld; and

(b) an acknowledgement from the parents, preferably in writing or before a witness, that the danger had been explained to them and that their consent was still withheld.'

Unfortunately there have been instances where Jehovah's Witness parents have rejected their child following a transfusion of blood given against their wishes. Doctors should bear this possibility in mind also when considering whether this sort of treatment should be given.

1.3   Transplantation of Organs and Tissue

1.3.1   Live Donors

Where the potential source is a live adult donor, full, free and informed consent for the removal of human tissue must be formally obtained as for all surgical procedures. In the case of minors then in the absence of any specific statutory authority or decided court cases it has been suggested that the general rules about consent also apply. (See Mason J K, McCall Smith R A, *Law and Medical Ethics*, 2nd Edition, London: Butterworths, 1987, p22.) The same writers also query whether parents can ever validly consent to medical treatment which is not in the interests of their child. Doctors would therefore be best advised to consult their defence organisations before accepting a child as a donor. In the White Paper *Advice from the Advisory Group on Transplantation Problems on the question of amending the Human Tissue Act 1961* (London: HMSO, 1969, Cmnd 4106) it is stated that: 'The propriety of using a live donor is a matter for the ethical judgement of the doctor in the circumstances governing each individual case'.

1.3.2 Dead Donors

If the transplanted organ is to be taken from a cadaver then the Human Tissue Act 1961 (not applicable in Northern Ireland where the situation is regulated by the Human Tissue Act (Northern Ireland) 1962) and the Corneal Tissue Act 1986 (not applicable in Northern Ireland) regulate the position.

Section 1(1) of the Human Tissue Act 1961 states: 'If any person, either in writing at any time or orally in the presence of two or more witnesses during his last illness, has expressed a request that his body or any specified part of his body be used after his death for therapeutic purposes or for the purposes of medical education or research, the person lawfully in possession of the body after his death may, unless he has reason to believe that the request was subsequently withdrawn, authorise the removal from the body of any part or, as the case may be, the specified part, for use in accordance with the request'.

It should be noted that there is no specific wording that the deceased must have used and the request can be made orally during a terminal illness if witnessed by at least two people. DHSS Circular HSC(IS)156 advises that those wishing to donate their bodies should be asked to make a written statement to that effect and to carry this on their person. Would-be donors should also be encouraged to discuss their wishes with their family or anyone close to them. Donors should be advised to take their donor card with them if ever admitted to hospital and if once there they tell staff that they have made such a request, or if they make one whilst in hospital, that fact should be included in the patient's medical records. Hospitals are warned that patients should not be pressed to complete donor cards although it is acceptable for a hospital to display posters and have kidney donor cards freely available.

The question of who is 'lawfully in possession' and may thus give the necessary authorisation has given rise to much debate. Is it the person or authority which has control over the premises in which the person died or is it the deceased's executor or next of kin? DHSS Circular HSC(IS)156 offers the following guidance:

'If a person dies in hospital, the person lawfully in possession of the body, at least until the executors or "relatives" ask for the body to be handed to them, is the Area Health Authority or the Board of Governors responsible for the hospital. In the case of a private institution or a Services hospital, the person lawfully in possession would be the managers and Commanding Officer respectively.'

'If a person dies elsewhere than in hospital the question of who is lawfully in possession should not normally give rise to difficulty. Thus, it may be the husband in the case of a deceased wife, the parent in the case of a deceased child, the executor, if any, or even the householder on whose premises the body lies. If a person is brought into hospital dead the Health Authority will be lawfully in possession of the body. . . , although in such cases the Coroner will normally be involved.'

In those cases where a body is lawfully in the possession of a hospital, nursing home or other institution the Act permits the managers to delegate the right to give authority to remove tissue under the Act to a designated person.

The person 'lawfully in possession' is under no obligation to authorise tissue removal even if the deceased made it clear that he wished this to be done. Thus the question of who has the right to make this authorisation could be important. There could in theory be a dispute between the hospital and the relatives as to which of them was 'lawfully in possession' for these purposes. In the book Mason JK, McCall Smith RA, *Law and Medical Ethics*, 2nd Edition, London: Butterworths, 1987, the authors state: 'We believe that to accede to the relatives in such circumstances would be the lesser of two evils but it is fortunate that such conflicts are very rare in practice.'

It must be noted that if a person has reason to believe that the coroner or procurator fiscal may require an inquest or inquiry or a post mortem to be held, tissue cannot be removed without the consent of the coroner or procurator fiscal. There is no statutory requirement that this consent be in writing. This applies equally if tissue is removed in the circumstances set out below.

The second set of circumstances in which tissue may be removed under the Human Tissue Act 1961 is specified in Section 1(2). This states that the person lawfully in possession (see discussion above) of the body can authorise the removal of any part of the body for the same purposes as mentioned above if 'having made such reasonable enquiry as may be practicable, he has no reason to believe:

(a) that the deceased had expressed an objection to his body being so dealt with after his death, and had not withdrawn it; or

(b) that the surviving spouse or any surviving relative of the deceased objects to the body being so dealt with.'

The Act does not state what a reasonable enquiry should consist of but DHSS Circular HSC(IS)156 gives guidance on this point: '. . . in most instances it will be sufficient to discuss the matter with any one relative who had been in close contact with the deceased, asking him his own views, the views of the deceased and also if he has any reason to believe that any other relative would be likely to object. In certain circumstances it might be necessary for such discussion to take place on the telephone. Potential organ donors will often have spent some hours or even days in hospital and in such cases hospitals will have sufficient opportunity to take steps to contact relatives. Where after such reasonable enquiry as may be practicable there is no evidence that the donor has any relatives, authority may be given under Section 1(2) in the absence of any other evidence which suggests to the contrary. Where it is known that a potential donor has relatives but it has not been possible to contact any of them, a person giving authority for organ removal must be especially careful to ensure that the requirements of the Act with regard to the making of enquiries have been met. It is not enough to say in a case where organs must be removed very soon after death that no enquiry is practicable. Any objections made by patient or relatives should be noted immediately in the patient's notes. The word ''relatives'' is not defined in the Act, but there are some circumstances in which it ought to be interpreted in the widest sense, eg to include those who although claiming only a distant relationship are nevertheless closely concerned with the deceased.'

As long as the terms of the statute are adhered to there is no legal requirement that relatives consent in writing to tissue removal. However, DHSS Circular HC(77)28 states in relation to proposed removal of tissue for transplant purposes at post mortems that the Department 'considers it desirable' that relatives should be invited to sign a post mortem declaration form. The form contains a consent to remove 'amounts of tissue for the treatment of other patients and for medical education and research'. The Circular also states however that 'it is accepted that there will be occasions when only verbal enquiry is possible'.

If the deceased was known to have a particular religion then consultation with an appropriate religious leader might well be advisable. Some Hindus, for example, might object to organ removal after death, and in Judaism, as the question of when life is extinct might not accord with that given below, the deceased person might have objected to organ removal.

When it comes to the removal of the organs Section 1(4) of the Human Tissue Act 1961, as amended by the Corneal Tissue Act 1986, states: 'No such removal, except of eyes, or parts of eyes shall be effected except by a registered medical practitioner who must have satisfied himself by personal examination of the body that life is extinct'. Section 1(4)(A) states that eyes or parts of eyes can only be removed as above or by 'a person in the employment of a health authority acting on the instructions of a registered medical practitioner who must, before giving those instructions, be satisfied that the person in question is sufficiently qualified and trained to perform the removal competently and must also either -

    i   have satisfied himself by personal examination of the body that life is extinct, or

    ii   be satisfied that life is extinct on the basis of a statement to that effect by a registered medical practitioner who has satisfied himself by personal examination of the body that life is extinct.'

1.3.3 Brain Death

There is no legal definition of death. In 1983 a revised edition of the *Code of Practice on the Removal of Cadaveric Organs for Transplantation* was drawn up by a Working Party on behalf of the Health Departments of Great Britain and Northern Ireland. This includes a section on diagnosis of death and reproduces the texts of the papers 'Diagnosis of Brain Death' and 'Diagnosis of Death' by the Conference of Royal Colleges and Faculties of the United Kingdom as appendices. The Code of Practice was commended to hospital doctors by the Chief Medical Officer in January 1980 (CMO(80)1).

1.4 Police and Criminal Evidence Act 1984

By virtue of the Police and Criminal Evidence Act 1984 doctors may be involved in performing intimate body searches and taking intimate body samples from persons in police custody. As this would normally constitute assault unless the person consented in the usual way, it is worth noting when such searches etc. are in fact lawful.

Section 55 deals with 'intimate searches' defined by Section 118 as 'a search which consists of physical examination of a person's body orifices'. Such a search of a person arrested and in police detention may be authorised by an officer of at least the rank of superintendent in certain listed circumstances. One such is that the prisoner may have a Class A drug (see Schedule to Misuse of Drugs Act under subchapter 3.5.2, Supply) concealed on his person and was in possession of same with the appropriate criminal intent before arrest. A search on these grounds must be carried out by a registered medical practitioner or a state registered nurse (SRN). Other searches should be carried out this way too unless a police officer of at least the rank of superintendent considers that this is not practicable, in which case a police officer must perform the search. The other grounds on which such a search can be authorised are that the prisoner may have concealed on him anything which he could use to cause physical injury to himself or others and which he might so use while he is in police detention or in the custody of the court.

Section 62 deals with the taking of intimate samples from persons in police detention. Section 65 defines an intimate sample as a 'sample of blood, semen or any other tissue fluid, urine, saliva or pubic hair, or a swab taken from a person's body orifice'. All such samples except for urine or saliva must be taken by a registered medical practitioner and either the consent of the prisoner must be obtained or the authorisation of a police officer of at least the rank of superintendent. The consent needed is that of the prisoner if he has attained the age of 17, but if he has not but has attained the age of 14 not only his consent but that of his parent or guardian is also required. If the prisoner is under 14 the parent's or guardian's consent only is required. If the consent is not forthcoming then a senior police officer may authorise the taking of the sample only if he has reasonable grounds:

'(a) for suspecting the involvement of the person . . . in a serious arrestable offence; and

(b) for believing that the sample will tend to confirm or disprove his involvement.'

1.5 Emergency Treatment: the Unconscious Patient

In the introductory paragraph it was explained that a doctor should not treat a patient without the latter's consent. However, a patient might be brought into hospital unconscious, urgently needing treatment but in no fit state to consent to anything. In such a situation it is considered that any doctor who went ahead and treated the unconscious patient could not later be sued or prosecuted for assault. This is because the common law defence of necessity is considered to be applicable to such situations.

Another argument put forward is that a patient's consent could be inferred from the surrounding circumstances, ie that any reasonable person would want the doctor to do everything necessary to save his life or to minimise the effects of the accident in question.

It must be noted, however, that two important limitations attach to this exception to the law of consent.

1   Doctors should not treat the patient if it is clearly known and stated that the latter would, if conscious, object to the treatment. For example, a Jehovah's Witness (see subchapter 1.2) and any patient who had previously stated that if readmitted to hospital he did not consent to further treatment.

2   The doctor should not give the patient more extensive treatment than is necessary to cope with the particular emergency.

It might in any event be advisable to get the next of kin to consent on the unconscious patient's behalf if possible.

1.6 The Patient with Mental Illness or Mental Handicap

The subject 'mental illness' is discussed in subchapter 5.5, which covers the provisions in the Mental Health Act 1983 which deal with the procedures which must be followed before a patient can lawfully be given certain types of treatment for mental illness. There appears to be no provision in the Act for an appropriate person to consent to other forms of medical treatment (eg removal of cataracts) on behalf of a patient too ill to be able to consent for himself. Brief reference is made to the power to receive mentally ill patients into guardianship and the effect of same. Although the guardian can insist that the patient attend at a particular place for, amongst other things, medical treatment there is no right for the guardian to consent to medical treatment on behalf of the patient. The absence of such a right has given rise to difficulties.

In the case of minors, ie those under 18, the issue can be dealt with by commencing wardship proceedings and asking leave of a High Court judge to carry out the operation in question. This was done in the case of Re B (A Minor) (Wardship) Sterilisation CA 16.3.87. That case related to a mentally retarded minor placed in the care of the local authority. It was considered that other forms of contraception were unsuitable and therefore the court's leave was sought for a sterilisation operation. The judge granted the order but he did make it clear that High Court permission ought to be sought in such circumstances even if the minor is under 16. In this case the girl was 17. (See subchapter 1.2, Jehovah's Witnesses, for the different legal position of minors over as opposed to those under 16.)

The law moved forward in the case of Re T 10.7.87 Wood J, *The Times*, July 11, 1987. There the High Court was asked to sanction the abortion and sterilisation of a severely handicapped woman who was aged 19 and thus too old to be a ward of court (maximum age is 18). The judge granted declarations that the surgeon who performed these two operations would not be acting unlawfully in so doing. He did so on the basis that there were exceptional circumstances where the law did not provide for consent, and the patient was suffering such mental abnormality that she was unable to consent for herself. Therefore in these circumstances a medical practitioner was justified in taking such steps as good medical practice demanded.

It would appear, therefore, that a doctor may be able to treat a patient too ill to consent *but the sanction of the High Court must first be obtained.*

2 Confidentiality

2.1 Introduction: the Duty Owed

There is no doubt that a doctor owes a duty of confidentiality to those who consult him. Any breach of that duty could result in disciplinary proceedings. Whether the aggrieved patient could successfully sue in the civil courts is a matter of some debate but any medical practitioner who risked putting this to the test would be extremely ill advised.

At present there is no statutory right to sue another person for damages for breach of confidentiality. However, the Law Commission in their report *Breach of Confidence* (1981 – Cmnd 8388) recommended that, as the common law action for breach of confidence is ineffective, it should be replaced by a statutory offence to include 'such usual confidences as arise between doctor and patient' (para 6.1). In addition, that it should be extended to reports passing between general practitioners and specialists. For now the legal position can only be defined from a study of decided court cases and academic comment. It is generally considered that professional people, including doctors, do owe a legal duty of confidentiality to those who consult them. The legal remedies of those aggrieved by any breach of such duty are thought to be severely limited. The Law Commission, for instance, in their report state that in most cases it would not be possible to claim damages for mental distress although a claim for economic loss might well succeed.

There is doubt additionally as to what, if any, legal duty of confidentiality is owed to the dead. The Law Commission in their report are of the opinion that the deceased's executors could only sue in relation to a breach of confidence after death if the 'information is of a "quasi-proprietal" character – such as information relating to "know-how" – which can be regarded as an asset of the deceased's estate'.

In their April 1987 blue booklet (paras 78–87) the GMC make it clear that a doctor is under a duty 'strictly to observe the rule of professional secrecy by refraining from disclosing voluntarily to any third party information about a patient which he has learnt directly or indirectly in his professional capacity as a registered medical practitioner'. The GMC go on to say that 'the death of the patient does not absolve the doctor from this obligation' but later the extent to which disclosure after death is regarded as improper is considered. It is stated this will depend on a 'number of factors' and examples are given, ie the nature of the information disclosed, the extent to which same has already appeared in published material, and the circumstances surrounding the disclosure including the period which has elapsed since the patient's death. The GMC are not prepared to give a time limit after which the disclosure would be considered proper. The ethical position is, therefore, quite clear and readers should also refer to the BMA *Handbook of Medical Ethics* (paras 1.5–1.21).

If one of the exceptions detailed below apply, a doctor may be justified in breaching the general duty of confidentiality, but the warning in the GMC April 1987 blue booklet (para 82) should still be heeded:

'Whatever the circumstances, a doctor must always be prepared to justify his action if he has disclosed confidential information. If a doctor is in doubt whether any of the exceptions mentioned above would justify him in disclosing information in a particular situation he will be wise to seek advice from a medical defence society or professional association.'

The main exceptions are the following:

1 Consent by patient to disclosure.
2 Order of court to disclose. (See subchapter 2.2.3.)
3 Statutory duty – notifiable diseases. (See subchapter 2.3.)
4 Statutory duty – other. (See subchapter 3.5.)
5 Disclosure to the family in the interests of the patient. (See subchapter 2.4.)
6 Disclosure to other third parties in the interests of the patient. (See subchapter 2.4.1.)
7 Sharing information with other health professionals. (See subchapter 2.6.)
8 Disclosure for research purposes.

Three other topics should also be considered in this context:

9 The extent to which a doctor may be justified in informing the authorities when he becomes aware that a patient has committed a serious crime. (See subchapter 2.5.)
10 The extent to which police officers investigating a crime may be justified in seizing medical records. (See subchapter 2.7.)
11 Doctors employed in the prison service, armed forces or in occupational medicine may find their duty of confidentiality to the patient conflicts with their duty to their employer. (See chapter 5; 1,2 and 3.)

2.2 Court Proceedings

2.2.1 General

There is no rule of law to the effect that a doctor cannot be ordered by a court of law to reveal confidential information obtained by him in the course of his work. If a doctor were to be ordered by a court to reveal such information and then did so, no legal action for breach of any duty of confidentiality could later be brought against the doctor on that basis. The GMC would also not subject a doctor to disciplinary proceedings if the breach of confidence took place because a court of law ordered a doctor to disclose confidential information. Conversely, if a doctor decided to defy an order of the court he might later be found to be in 'contempt of court' and as a result of such a finding the doctor could suffer severe penalties. This situation demonstrates how the rule of law can sometimes conflict with medical ethics.

2.2.2 Pre-trial Disclosure of Documents

For some time there has been a court rule to the effect that once a civil legal action has been commenced in the courts all the parties to it must at some stage before the actual hearing produce to each other all documents which they have in their 'possession, custody or power' which are relevant to the issues and not privileged (ie immune) from production. The subject of ownership and retention of health records is dealt with under chapter 10, Medical Records. In the case of National Health Service (NHS) hospital records these are considered to be in the custody of the relevant health authority, to whom applications for disclosure should be properly directed. NHS general practice records, although the property of the Secretary of State, would usually be in the custody of the general practitioner. Private practice records would likewise be in the custody of the medical practitioner, but employees' health records would be in the custody of the occupational health physician.

Medical records are not privileged in this context (but the court might limit their production to selected persons). Medical reports prepared in con-templation of litigation are privileged from production provided that it can be established that the sole or dominant purpose for which the document was prepared was in fact to submit same to a legal adviser in anticipation of possible court proceedings. Medical reports prepared in connection with the case in question are also privileged. However, if it is desired to call the writer of any expert report to give oral evidence then the court will order that the report must first be shown to the other side, unless there are special reasons for not doing so. (Order 38 Rule 37 of the Rules of the Supreme Court.)

Order 38 Rule 38 of the Rules of the Supreme Court provides for a direction as appropriate for medical experts to meet and identify the main issues.

Note also that an English court case has decided that, if on balance it would not be in the public interest to order a party to reveal a document then that party can be excused from doing so. The case was D v NSPCC [1978] AC 171. A parent started a court case against the National Society for the Prevention of Cruelty to Children (NSPCC) and applied for an order requiring the organisation to disclose confidential records to the parent. Information which proved to be unfounded had been given to the NSPCC to the effect that the parent had been mistreating her children and the parent wanted to find out who the informer was. The court declined to order disclosure on the basis that to do so would be contrary to the public interest in that other informers would be deterred from passing information to the NSPCC if they did not have the security of knowing that their identities would be kept secret.

Statute has extended the circumstances in which persons in possession of documents can be ordered to disclose them for the purposes of litigation. It is possible even before an action has been commenced for a doctor to be ordered to disclose medical records, although in England and Wales this applies only if the doctor is likely to be made a party to the contemplated litigation. The relevant powers are contained in Section 33(2) of the Supreme Court Act 1981, Section 52(2) of the County Court Act 1984 and the Administration of Justice (Scotland) Act 1972 Section 1. The court should make the order only if the documents are likely to be relevant to the proposed claim. The proceedings must be in the civil courts and in England and Wales must relate to a claim for personal injuries or a death. Also in England and Wales the court may attach conditions to the order to disclose and may direct that disclosure be to the claimant or limited to his legal, medical or other professional adviser. The usual rules about privilege still apply.

The same statutes also provide that a third party, not involved in the litigation, can be ordered to produce relevant documents. In England and Wales the litigation must have actually begun and the order can be made on the same conditions as set out above.

Note that the GMC blue booklet of April 1987 states (para 81 (f)) '. . . where litigation is in prospect, unless the patient has consented to disclosure, or a formal court order has been made for disclosure, information should not be disclosed merely in response to demands from other persons such as another party's solicitor or an official of the court'. In other words, even though the doctor is made aware that a power to order disclosure exists the doctor should still wait for a formal court order before disclosing any information in circumstances where the patient objects to the disclosure being made.

2.2.3 Evidence in Court

A doctor may be summoned to attend court to give evidence and to produce medical records at the same time. Any subpoena or witness summons should be accompanied by 'conduct money' (to pay the witness' fares to court) and the doctor is entitled to be paid an allowance for attending (the amount of this allowance is fixed in accordance with prescribed rates which change from time to time). If a doctor were to fail to attend court when summoned this could amount to a contempt of court.

Once in the witness box, if the doctor is asked a question which he does not wish to answer on the grounds that this would breach his duty of confidentiality then it is open to the doctor to ask the judge for permission to be excused from answering the question on this ground, but if the judge orders the doctor to answer questions then the doctor legally must do so because to refuse could amount to contempt of court. For example, in the course of one divorce case a psychiatrist who had been consulted by the wife and co-respondent was subpoenaed by the husband's legal advisors. Once in court he was asked by the husband's counsel to reveal what the wife and co-respondent had said to him during the consultation. The psychiatrist protested on the grounds of professional confidence but the judge ruled that he must answer the questions or be committed to prison for contempt of court. Not surprisingly he then gave evidence. (Nuttall v Nuttall and Twyman [1964] 108 Sol J 605.) The court stated that if the psychiatrist had refused and had appealed against the direction to disclose the evidence the court of appeal might have upheld him. However that statement was queried in the D v NSPCC case (D v NSPCC [1987] AC 171) (see subchapter 2.2.2). This rule has been held to apply even in circumstances where a doctor is under a statutory duty to keep the information in question confidential.

The subject of privilege has been dealt with during the past 20 years by both the Law Reform Committee (16th Report *Privilege in Legal Proceedings*, 1967, Cmnd 3472) and the Criminal Law Revision Committee (11th Report, *Evidence – General*, 1972, Cmnd 4991).

The BMA advises doctors to initially refuse to answer questions in court if they do not have their patient's permission but states that if disclosure is ordered 'the decision whether to comply or not must be for his own conscience' (*Handbook of Medical Ethics* (para 1.16).) The GMC state (para 81(f) of the blue booklet) that a doctor may disclose information if so directed by a judge or other presiding officer of a court or if summoned by the authority of a court in Scotland.

2.2.4 Inquiries Following a Death

The GMC also state (para 81(f)) that a doctor may give information to a coroner or his nominated representative to the extent necessary to enable a coroner to determine whether an inquest should be held. Also, if summoned to appear before a procurator fiscal in Scotland under the latter's power to investigate sudden suspicious deaths the doctor may disclose information.

2.3 Notifiable Diseases

In some cases the doctor's general duty of confidentiality is overridden by a statutory duty to notify the authorities that a patient is suffering from a particular infectious disease. In England and Wales the law on this subject is presently contained in the Public Health (Control of Disease) Act 1984 and various Regulations.

Under the Act a registered medical practitioner who becomes aware or who suspects that a patient whom he is attending within the district of a local authority is suffering from what the Act terms a 'notifiable disease' or food poisoning must send to the proper officer of that local authority the appropriate certificate unless he has reasonable grounds for believing that some other registered medical practitioner has already done so.

The certificate must state:

(a) The name, age, sex and address of the patient;

(b) The disease from which the patient is, or is suspected to be suffering, and the date or approximate date of its onset; and

(c) If the patient is in a hospital, the day on which the patient was admitted, the address of the premises from which he came there and whether or not, in the opinion of the person giving the certificate, the disease or poisoning was contracted in the hospital.

The certificates are available to registered medical practitioners on request, free of charge. The practitioner receives a fee on notifying the authorities.

Under the Act failure to comply with this duty could result in a criminal prosecution, the penalty being a fine.

Further powers exist under the Act in respect of those suffering from notifiable diseases. Sections 35 and 36 provide for compulsory examination of those suspected of suffering from or being carriers of notifiable diseases.

Section 35 states that if a Justice of the Peace (JP) has received a written certificate issued by a registered medical practitioner nominated by the local authority and is satisfied:

'(a) that there is reason to believe that some person in the district

    i   is or has been suffering from a notifiable disease, or

    ii   though not suffering from such a disease, is carrying an organism that is capable of causing it, and

(b) that in his own interest, or in the interest of his family, or in the public interest, it is expedient that he should be medically examined, and

(c) that he is not under the treatment of a registered medical practitioner or that the registered medical practitioner who is treating him consents to the making of an order . . .'

then the court may order such an examination. The Act states that the examination may include subjecting the patient to bacteriological and radiological tests and similar investigations.

Similarly Section 36 provides that compulsory medical examinations can be imposed on groups of persons if the group is believed to comprise carriers of notifiable diseases.

The JP must be satisfied:

'(a) that there is reason to believe that one of a group of persons, though not suffering from a notifiable disease, is carrying an organism that is capable of causing it, and

(b) that in the interests of those persons or their families, or in the public interest, it is expedient that those persons should be medically examined.'

Section 37 of the Act provides for the compulsory removal to hospital of those suffering from notifiable diseases. If, on the application of a local authority, a JP is of the opinion that a person is suffering from a notifiable disease and that proper precautions to prevent the spread of infection cannot be or are not being taken and that same is causing a serious risk of infection to others then the JP may order the person's removal to hospital provided there is space available for him and the District Health Authority consents.

Under Section 38 if a JP is of the opinion that the patient '. . . would not on leaving the hospital be provided with lodging or accommodation in which proper precautions could be taken to prevent the spread of the disease by him' the JP may order further detention in hospital for as long as is necessary in his opinion. A patient thus detained would be guilty of an offence if he discharged himself.

It should be noted that Sections 35, 36, 37 and 38 all provide that 'if he deems it necessary' the JP may act *ex parte*. This means the JP may make these orders without the person affected thereby being present in court or represented.

The Act makes many other provisions in respect of notifiable disease. These include the prosecution of those who, knowing that they suffer from a notifiable disease, act in such a way as to expose others to risk of infection (Section 17). Also persons with notifiable diseases can be stopped from trading (Section 19) and persons with notifiable diseases can be forced to stop working (Section 20). This would affect, for instance, those involved in the preparation of food. (Such people are entitled to Statutory Sick Pay if they are eligible under the Social Security and Housing Benefits Act 1982 and also compensation according to the Public Health (Control of Disease) Act 1984.)

2.3.1 List of Notifiable Diseases

The following diseases are 'notifiable' by virtue of the 1984 Act.

Cholera
Plague
Relapsing Fever
Smallpox
Typhus

Those below are 'notifiable' under the Public Health (Infectious Diseases) Regulations 1968 as amended.

Acute Encephalitis	Malaria
Acute Meningitis	Marburg Disease
Acute Poliomyelitis	Measles
Amoebic Dysentery	Ophthalmia Neonatorum
Anthrax	Paratyphoid Fever
Bacillary Dysentery	Rabies
Diphtheria	Scarlet Fever
Food Poisoning or	Tetanus
suspected food poisoning	Tuberculosis
Infective Jaundice	Typhoid Fever
Leprosy	Viral Haemorrhagic Fever
Leptospirosis	Whooping Cough
Lassa Fever	Yellow Fever

Public Health (Infectious Diseases) Regulations 1985 (S.I. 1985 No.434) (introduced in March 1985) apply certain provisions of the 1984 Act to the Acquired Immune Deficiency Syndrome (AIDS) but do not make it compulsorily notifiable. The provisions which apply to AIDS are Section 35 (medical examination), and Section 37 (removal to hospital) (see above for both), and Section 38 (detention in hospital) (see above again) but note that Section 38 is modified in the case of AIDS to permit an order to be made:

'. . . if the Justice is satisfied that on his (the patient's) leaving hospital proper precautions to prevent the spread of that disease would not be taken by him -

(a) in his lodging or accommodation, or

(b) in other places to which he may be expected to go if not detained in the hospital.'

In Scotland the Statute Law has been consolidated and the law is to be found in a number of statutes extending back to the Infectious Diseases (Notification) Act 1889. Sections 54 to 58 of the Public Health (Scotland) Act 1897 as amended contain similar provisions to Sections 17, 19, 20, 37 and 38 of the 1984 English Act and in addition make it an offence to send a child to school with an infectious disease. Notification is to be made by a general practitioner who becomes aware that a patient is suffering from an infectious disease to the Chief Administrative Medical Officer of the local Health Board (National Health Service (Scotland) Act 1972 – Schedule 6).

The Health Services and Public Health Act 1968 Sections 71 to 74 provide powers under the order of the Sheriff for compulsory medical examination of individuals or groups in similar circumstances to those provided by Sections 35 and 36 of the English Statute.

Although AIDS is not a notifiable infectious disease in Scotland, there are powers under the Public Health (Scotland) Act 1897 Sections 45 to 59 to provide for the compulsory examination of those suspected of any infectious disease and, if necessary, for their compulsory removal to hospital. The following infectious diseases are compulsorily notifiable in Scotland by regulations made by the Secretary of State for Scotland:

Anthrax	Plague
Cholera	Poliomyelitis, acute, paralytic
Continued Fever	Poliomyelitis, acute, non-paralytic
Diphtheria	Puerperal Fever
Dysentery	Rabies
Erysipelas	Relapsing Fever
Lassa Fever	Scarlet Fever
Leprosy	Smallpox
Leptospiral Jaundice	Tuberculosis, respiratory
Malaria	Tuberculosis, non-respiratory
Marburg Disease	Typhoid Fever
Measles	Typhus Fever
Membranous Croup	Viral Hepatitis
Meningococcal Infection	Viral Haemorrhagic Fever
Ophthalmia Neonatorum	Whooping Cough
Paratyphoid A	Yellow Fever
Paratyphoid B	

Food poisoning is notifiable under the Food and Drugs (Scotland) Act 1956.

It is also worth noting the provisions of the National Health Service (Venereal Diseases) Regulations (S.I. 1974 No.29) (England and Wales only) which impose a statutory obligation on health authorities to take steps to prevent the identification of individuals who have been treated for any sexually transmitted disease.

Regulation 2 requires '. . . every Regional and District Health Authority to take all necessary steps to secure that any information capable of identifying an individual obtained by officers of the Authority with respect to persons examined or treated for any sexually transmitted disease shall not be disclosed except

(a) for the purpose of communicating that information to a medical practitioner, or to a person employed under the direction of a medical practitioner in connection with the treatment of persons suffering from such disease or the prevention of the spread thereof, and

(b) for the purpose of such treatment or prevention.'

2.4 Disclosure to the Family and to Non-relatives

There are two situations where this may be justified: firstly where in the circumstances it is considered undesirable to tell the patient the full implications of his condition, and secondly where a doctor is consulted by a person under the age of 16.

The GMC blue booklet (para 81 (c)) states the following: 'If in particular circumstances the doctor believes it undesirable on medical grounds to seek the patient's consent, information regarding the patient's health may sometimes be given in confidence to a close relative or person in a similar relationship to the patient'.

This is, however, expressly stated to be qualified by the following guidance concerning patients under the age of 16 set out in paragraphs 83-85. These paragraphs were redrafted following the much publicised court case Gillick v West Norfolk and Wisbech Area Health Authority and the DHSS [1985] 3 WLR 830 3 AER 402. Mrs Gillick, who had five daughters, sought an assurance from her local AHA that they would not give advice and treatment concerning contraception to her daughters whilst they were under the age of 16 without her prior knowledge or consent. Failing to receive such an assurance she applied to the court for amongst other things a declaration that the AHA could not lawfully give such advice or treatment as being against the law relating to parental rights. The case eventually reached the House of Lords where the decision on this point was that parental rights were recognised by law only as long as they were needed for the protection of the child and such rights yielded to the child's right to his own decisions when reaching sufficient understanding and intelligence so as to be capable of making up his own mind. Therefore a girl under 16 did not by virtue of her age lack legal capacity to consent to contraceptive advice and treatment by a doctor. The doctor has a discretion to give contraceptive advice or treatment without the parents' knowledge and consent to a girl under 16 provided the girl has reached an age where she has a sufficient understanding and intelligence to enable her to understand fully what is proposed, that being a question of a fact in each case.

The GMC now state the following:

'83. Where a child below the age of 16 consults a doctor for advice or treatment, and is not accompanied at the consultation by a parent or a person *in loco parentis*, the doctor must particularly have in mind the need to foster and maintain parental responsibility and family stability. Before offering advice or treatment the doctor should satisfy himself, after careful assessment, that the child has sufficient maturity and understanding to appreciate what is involved. For example, if the request is for treatment for a pregnancy or contraceptive advice, the doctor should satisfy himself that the child has sufficient appreciation of what is involved in relation to his or her emotional development, family relationships, problems associated with the impact of pregnancy and/or its termination and the potential risks to health of sexual intercourse and certain forms of contraception at an early age.

84. If the doctor is satisfied of the child's maturity and ability to understand as set out above, he must nonetheless seek to persuade the child to involve a parent, or another person *in loco parentis*, in the consultation. If the child nevertheless refuses to allow a parent or such other person to be told, the doctor must decide, in the patient's best medical interests, whether or not to offer advice or treatment. He should, however, respect the rules of professional confidentiality set out above in the foregoing paragraphs of this section.

24

85. If the doctor is not so satisfied, he may decide to disclose the information learned from the consultation; but if he does so he should inform the patient accordingly, and his judgement concerning disclosure must always reflect both the patient's best medical interests and the trust the patient places in the doctor.'

The BMA gives the following advice to doctors where a girl under the age of 16 requests contraception but refuses to allow her parents to be informed:

(a) Attempt to convince the girl of the advisability of involving her parents in this decision. This should be part of the counselling extended over a number of interviews, where appropriate. In many cases the doctor will gain consent to involve a parent or a person *in loco parentis.*

(b) If he is unsuccessful, the doctor must then decide whether the girl has the mental maturity to understand his advice and the possible consequences of her action. If she has not, then her consent is not informed and so invalid. The doctor cannot provide treatment in these circumstances but should keep confidential the fact and content of the consultation.

(c) If he is satisfied that she can consent, he makes a clinical decision as to whether the provision of contraception is in the best interests of the patient.

(d) A decision not to prescribe does not absolve him from keeping the interview confidential.

It is only in those cases, therefore, where the under-age patient does not have the necessary capacity to understand, that the doctor may be justified in telling his or her parents what has occurred at the consultation. However, the doctor must tell the patient what he proposes to do and must consider also the patient's best medical interests and the trust that was placed in the doctor. Where the doctor decides to tell the under-age patient's parents, he must be prepared to justify his actions.

2.4.1   *Disclosure to Third Parties in the Interests of the Patient*

Para 81 (d) of the GMC blue booklet states:

'If in the doctor's opinion disclosure of information to a third party other than a relative would be in the best interests of the patient, it is the doctor's duty to make every reasonable effort to persuade the patient to allow the information to be given. If the patient still refuses then only in exceptional cases should the doctor feel entitled to disregard his refusal.'

2.5   Serious Crime

If a doctor were faced with a patient suffering with a gunshot wound, for example, the doctor might well have reason to suspect that the patient had sustained this injury whilst engaged in the commission of a crime. Conversely the doctor might know this for certain because the patient might admit that this was how the injury was obtained. Would the doctor then be under some sort of a duty to report the existence of the injury to the police and if he did decide to do so what repercussions might there be?

The general position is that it is not a criminal offence not to reveal information to the police about a crime. In England and Wales Section 5(5) of the Criminal Law Act 1967 sets this out. Indeed in the English case of Rice v Connolly [1966] 2 QB 414 where a man charged with the offence of obstructing the police in the execution of their duty following his refusal to give any information about himself was found not guilty, Lord Justice Parker stated: 'It seems to me quite clear that though every citizen has a moral duty or, if you like, a social duty to assist the police there is no legal duty to that effect'.

While not in the category of serious crime, an example of a case where the doctor's duty to society overrides his medical duty of confidentiality was that of Hunter v Mann [1974] QB 767 which related to a doctor's statutory obligation to supply information to the police about the identity of persons injured in a road accident.

However, to the general rule there are various exceptions.

2.5.1   Treason

It still is a common law offence in England and Wales for a person who knows or has reasonable cause to believe that another has committed treason to omit to disclose this information or any material part of it to the proper authority within a reasonable time.

In Scotland also the offence of misprision of treason still exists. This consists in the failure by anyone who has any information that might lead to the arrest of a traitor to give that information to the authorities. It might also be misprision to fail to give information of a projected treason.

2.5.2   Terrorism

Under the Prevention of Terrorism (Temporary Provisions) Act 1984 failure to give information about certain acts of terrorism could result in prosecution. This is set out in Section 11 of the Act which covers only acts of terrorism connected with Northern Irish affairs. An 'act of terrorism' in this context is defined in Section 14(1) as: 'the use of violence for political ends, and includes any use of violence for the purpose of putting the public or any section of the public in fear'.

Section 11 provides that a person can be guilty of a criminal offence in the following circumstances. Firstly 'if he has information which he knows or believes might be of material assistance -

    (a) in preventing the commission by any other person of an act of terrorism; or

(b) in securing the apprehension, prosecution or conviction of any other person for an offence involving the commission, preparation or instigation of an act of terrorism.'

And secondly if he 'fails without reasonable excuse to disclose that information as soon as reasonably practicable

    i   In England and Wales to a constable;

    ii In Scotland to a constable or the procurator fiscal; or

    iii In Northern Ireland to a constable or a member of Her Majesty's Forces.'

The penalties if a prosecution takes place in a higher court could be up to five years in prison and/or a fine.

2.5.3 Repercussions of Reporting a Crime

If a doctor did decide to report a patient to the police, what repercussions would there be? The legal position regarding breach of confidentiality is, as explained, far from clear and all that can be said is that no doctor has been sued successfully for reporting a patient for committing a crime.

Another area of concern for a doctor might be the possibility of disciplinary proceedings being brought by the GMC. Paragraph 81 (g) of the blue booklet states: 'Rarely disclosure may be justified on the ground that it is in the public interest which, in certain circumstances such as, for example, investigation by the police of a grave or very serious crime, might override the doctor's duty to maintain his patient's confidence'. As stated above, the GMC points out that any breach of confidence must be justified and doctors are advised to consult their defence organisations or professional organisations when in doubt. The BMA *Handbook of Medical Ethics* also gives advice (paras 1.11–1.13).

2.6 Sharing Information with Other Health Professionals

There may be circumstances in which a doctor wishes to disclose confidential information about a patient to other health professionals in order to provide optimum care. An obvious example would be a doctor admitting a patient with an infectious disease to hospital. Is a doctor justified in breaching confidence in this type of situation, and if so, to what extent?

The GMC, in their blue booklet, state at para 81 (b):

'Confidential information may be shared with other registered medical practitioners who participate in or assume responsibility for clinical management of the patient. To the extent that the doctor deems it necessary for the performance of their particular duties, confidential information may also be shared with other persons (nurses and other health care professionals) who are assisting and collaborating with the doctor in his professional relationship with the patient. It is the doctor's responsibility to ensure that such individuals appreciate that the information is being imparted in strict professional confidence.'

It is further stated at para 88:

'. . . Where one doctor shares confidential information with another doctor, the interests of the patient require that the doctor with whom the information is shared must observe the same rule of professional secrecy as the doctor who originally obtained the information from the patient.'

The GMC therefore regard the sharing of information as permissible when the doctor, as a matter of clinical judgement, perceives it to be in the patient's interests. It is necessary to draw a distinction between the situation where a doctor discloses without seeking express permission, and the situation where permission is sought but a patient refuses to allow disclosure.

If a patient has not specifically been asked whether he objects to his doctor passing information on to other health professionals, a court would probably infer consent, in that by submitting himself to a doctor's care, the patient impliedly accepts any steps the doctor may take in his best interests. This would not, however, justify a doctor disclosing confidential information to other health professionals at random. The criterion for disclosure must be a narrowly defined 'need to know' basis, ie only disclosure so far as is required to provide optimum care. Disclosing to someone outside that group would certainly be an unjustifiable breach. May a doctor rely on therapeutic privilege where a patient has expressly refused permission to disclose? The answer is probably not. What a doctor must do, however, is point out to the patient that unless he is able to share the information with other health professionals, his capability to treat him as comprehensively as he would like would be severely limited, and he should urge the patient to reconsider.

If the patient still adamantly refuses, the doctor must respect his feelings and maintain confidentiality. He should endeavour to treat the patient medically as far as is possible without disclosure. A doctor who refuses to treat in these circumstances could be negligently failing in his duty of care towards his patient.

2.7 Police and Criminal Evidence Act 1984

2.7.1 Confidentiality

Whilst the Police and Criminal Evidence Act 1984 was progressing through Parliament there was considerable debate as to whether police officers investigating alleged criminal offences should be permitted in the course of their investigations to seize a person's medical records. The resulting provisions of the Act provide that they may do so in only a very limited number of situations.

Section 8 of the Act sets out what power magistrates have to authorise police officers to enter premises and search therein. The warrant may be granted only if 'there are reasonable grounds for believing that a serious arrestable offence' (there is not space here to define this phrase precisely) 'has been committed; and that there is material on the premises' which does not come within the listed categories but is likely to be relevant evidence *and* it is not practicable to communicate with the person entitled to grant entry to the premises or access to the material *or* entry would not be granted voluntarily *or* the purposes of the search may be frustrated or seriously prejudiced unless a constable arriving at the premises can secure immediate entry to them.

One of the three listed categories referred to above, ie one sort of material that magistrates may not grant a warrant to search for, is what the Act terms 'excluded material'. This is defined in Section 11 to include:

'(a) Personal records which a person has acquired or created in the course of any trade, business, profession or other occupation or for the purposes of any paid or unpaid office and which he holds in confidence.'

'Personal records' are defined in Section 12 to include 'documentary and other records concerning an individual (whether living or dead) who can be identified from them and relating . . . to his physical or mental health'. The expression 'holds in confidence' is also defined (see below). Also included are the following:

'(b) Human tissue or tissue fluid which has been taken for the purposes of diagnosis or medical treatment and which a person holds in confidence.'

'Holds in confidence' is stated to mean being held subject to 'a) an express or implied undertaking to hold it in confidence; or b) to a restriction on disclosure or an obligation of secrecy contained in any enactment'.

There can be no doubt therefore that a patient's medical records would be classed as 'excluded material' for the purposes of the Police and Criminal Evidence Act 1984.

It is next necessary to consider in what circumstances police officers could, despite this classification, obtain such records. Section 9 states that a constable may apply to a circuit judge for such an order. Schedule 1 of the Act states the criteria that must apply. The application must be on notice and the judge must be satisfied that various listed 'access conditions' apply. These are:

1 There must be reasonable grounds for believing that there is excluded material on premises specified in the application.

2 There must be some statutory authority passed before the Police and Criminal Evidence Act which would have authorised such a search, and

3 The issue of a warrant under those provisions would have been appropriate.

Medical records could only be obtained by this method therefore if they could have been lawfully obtained by statute before the passing of the Police and Criminal Evidence Act. There were a number of statutes passed before the Police and Criminal Evidence Act which authorised the police to enter and search premises under warrant and in some cases seize documents, eg Misuse of Drugs Act 1971, Official Secrets Act 1911. There is not space here to list them all.

If the order is made it will be to the effect that the person who appears to be in possession of the excluded material shall produce same to the constable for him to take away or shall give the constable access to it. In certain circumstances the judge may grant a warrant to allow the constable to enter, search and seize excluded material. The above access conditions must be satisfied plus one extra condition similar to those set out for magistrates, ie connected with difficulties in communicating with the property owner, fears that serving a notice would seriously prejudice the investigation or that a notice has been served and disclosure of the material is feared.

There is another method by which, in theory, police could seize medical records. Section 19 provides a general power of seizure of documents etc to a constable who is lawfully on premises, ie either with the consent of the owner or by virtue of a warrant. Such a constable may, once inside, seize anything he finds if he has reasonable grounds to believe:

'(a) that it has been obtained in consequence of the commission of an offence; and

(b) that it is evidence in relation to an offence which he is investigating or any other offence; and

(c) that it is necessary to seize it in order to prevent the evidence being concealed, lost, altered or destroyed.'

There are also provisions requiring information held on computer to be produced. It follows from the above that a police officer who is lawfully inside premises could in theory seize medical records if he could justify doing same by virtue of the above criteria.

3 Drugs

3.1 Introduction

The law relating to drugs is complex and far reaching. In this chapter we deal with those aspects of the law which seem most likely to affect doctors in relation to: prescribing drugs, possession of drugs, supply and sale of drugs, import and export of drugs.

When considering the legal position it is always necessary to know how the term 'drug' is defined *vis-à-vis* the problem being considered. Some substances, eg heroin, cocaine and LSD are defined as 'controlled drugs'. Stringent restrictions exist stipulating who may and may not possess, supply, import and export controlled drugs. There are other substances which, although they may not be listed as a controlled drug, would be covered by the legal controls relating to what are termed 'medicinal products'. The legal definitions of a 'controlled drug' and a 'medicinal product' are listed in the glossary. Also set out is the legal definition of the term 'medicinal purpose' as it is necessary to know what this is to be able also to know what is meant by a 'medicinal product'.

When dealing with issues relating to import, export and commercial supply of drugs it will be noted that special provisions exist in relation to 'clinical trials'. The legal definition of a clinical trial also is reproduced in the glossary.

For reasons of convenience the following paragraphs are set out to detail firstly the law relating to possession, supply and prescription of controlled drugs. Next we consider the controls that exist in relation to medicinal products, the main bulk of the paragraphs being devoted to the complicated exemptions that exist in relation to the blanket prohibition against the sale on a commercial basis of such substances. Lastly the law relating to import and export of drugs is set out.

3.2 Possession and Supply of Controlled Drugs: the Criminal Law

The Misuse of Drugs Act 1971 provides that it is a criminal offence to manufacture, possess or supply to others 'controlled' drugs. However the Act also provides for Regulations to be made exempting certain persons from prosecution under these provisions.

The Misuse of Drugs Regulations (S.I. 1985 No.2066) provide in Regulations 8 and 9 that a 'practitioner' (this expression includes doctors who are *registered medical practitioners*) may while acting in his capacity as such 'manufacture or compound' and 'supply or offer to supply any drug specified in Schedules 2, or 5 to any person who may lawfully have that drug in his possession' notwithstanding the general prohibition in the Misuse of Drugs Act.

Regulation 7 provides that 'a doctor' (this again means registered doctor) 'or dentist may administer to a patient any drug specified in Schedules 2, 3, or 4 to the Regulations'. Any person may administer to another any drug specified in Schedule 5.

Under Regulation 10 a 'practitioner' may for the purpose of acting in 'his capacity as such', lawfully possess the drugs listed in Schedules 2 and 3. In the case of R v Dunbar [1982] 1 AER 188 it was held that a doctor *bona fide* treating himself is acting 'in his capacity as a doctor' for these purposes even though he is receiving the benefit of the drug himself. Anyone may possess the drugs listed in Schedule 5.

3.3 Prescribing Controlled Drugs

The same Regulations specify what details must be contained in prescriptions for 'controlled' drugs. (See glossary for Schedules listing the drugs controlled by these Regulations.) The Misuse of Drugs Act 1971 provides that breach of these Regulations is a criminal offence.

Under Regulation 16 prescriptions for controlled drugs other than those listed in Schedule 1 to these Regulations must satisfy the following criteria.

1   The prescription must be in ink or otherwise so as to be indelible and must be signed by the person issuing same with his usual signature and dated by him.

2   The prescription must, except in the case of health (ie National Health Service) prescriptions, specify the address of the person issuing same.

3   The prescription must specify in the doctor's own handwriting (the latter requirement does not apply though to prescriptions containing no controlled drugs other than phenobarbitone or phenobarbitone sodium) the following:

    i   name and address of the patient

    ii   the dose to be taken

    iii   'in the case of a prescription containing a controlled drug which is a preparation, the form and, where appropriate, the strength of the preparation and either the total quantity (in both words and figures) of the preparation or the number (in both words and figures) of dosage units, as appropriate, to be supplied', or in any other case the total quantity (in words and figures) of the controlled drug to be supplied.

(Current DHSS guidelines are unclear about whether the date needs to be in the doctor's handwriting. There have been cases where pharmacists have refused to dispense prescriptions not dated by hand, and clearer guidance is awaited.)

4   If the prescription is for a total quantity intended to be supplied by instalments it must contain a direction specifying the amount of the instalments of the total amount which may be supplied and the intervals to be observed when supplying.

3.4   Loss of the Right to Prescribe and Possess Controlled Drugs

The Misuse of Drugs Act 1971 also provides that doctors may, as a result of misconduct, be debarred from prescribing and in some circumstances from possessing controlled drugs. Section 12 of the Act states that if a doctor has been convicted of an offence under the Act then the Secretary of State may give a direction 'prohibiting him from having in his possession, prescribing, administering, manufacturing, compounding and supplying and from authorising the administration and supply of such controlled drugs as may be specified in the direction'.

A copy of the direction must be served on the doctor and notice of it published in the London, Edinburgh and Belfast Gazettes.

Other provisions in the Act provide that doctors who can be shown to have contravened Regulations made or licences granted under the Act's provisions or who have been prescribing controlled drugs in an irresponsible manner can also be made subject to a direction, in these cases prohibiting them from 'prescribing, administering and supplying and from authorising the administration and supply of such controlled drugs as may be specified in the direction'.

Before such a direction can be given and take effect the allegation must first be referred by the Secretary of State to, and be considered by, a tribunal and in some cases also an advisory body, both of which must be constituted in accordance with the Act. Details of the provisions are as follows.

3.4.1   Grounds for Reference to the Tribunal

There are three such:

i   Contravention of Misuse of Drugs Act Regulations.

See Section 13(1). The Regulations in question are those made under paragraphs (h) and (i) of Section 10(2) of the Act, ie Regulations which require doctors to give to the relevant authorities details of any patient whom they reasonably suspect to be addicted to controlled drugs and those which prohibit doctors from supplying such persons with controlled drugs except in accordance with a licence granted by virtue of the Act. (The Misuse of Drugs (Notification of, and Supply to Addicts) Regulations (S.I. 1973 No.799), as amended, referred to in subchapter 3.5 were passed under these provisions.)

ii Contravention of terms of a Misuse of Drugs Act licence.

See Section 13(1), ie a licence issued in accordance with Section 10(2) above.

iii Irresponsible prescribing.

See Section 13(2). If the Secretary of State is of the opinion that a doctor has been:

'prescribing, administering or supplying or authorising the administration or supply of any controlled drugs in an irresponsible manner' then the matter can be referred to the tribunal.

Section 16 of the Act states that the constitution and procedure of the tribunal are governed by the provisions of Schedule 3 of the Act. This provides, amongst other things, that the tribunal must have five members. One must be a lawyer of at least seven years' standing appointed by the Lord Chancellor and the other four are appointed by the Secretary of State and will be members of the medical profession who have been nominated by any of various listed bodies which include the GMC, the BMA and certain Royal Colleges.

The tribunal may decide that either there has been no contravention or misconduct, or that there has been such but that they do not recommend that any direction be given. If so, the Secretary of State must serve a notice to that effect on the doctor. (Section 14(3).)

If the tribunal decides that there has been a contravention or misconduct and that a direction should be given then the tribunal makes a recommendation to that effect and specifies which controlled drugs should be covered. (Section 14(4).) In that event the Secretary of State must then serve a notice on the doctor, stating whether or not he intends to give the recommended direction and, if so, stating the proposed terms of it. The doctor must also be informed of his right to make representations in writing to the Secretary of State within 28 days. (Section 14(5).)

If the Secretary of State receives any representations from the doctor within the 28 day period then he must refer same to an 'advisory body' which must advise the Secretary of State concerning whether or not a direction should be given. (Section 14(6).) The constitution and procedures of this body are also set out in Schedule 3. If the 28 days have expired or the Secretary of State has considered the advice of the advisory body then he may either give a direction, refer the matter back to the tribunal or order that no further proceedings be taken. (Section 14(7).) If a direction is given a copy of it must be served on the doctor and it must also be published in the London, Edinburgh and Belfast Gazettes.

Contravention of a direction given under either these provisions or those referred to above (ie under Section 12) is a criminal offence.

3.4.2 Temporary Directions

Section 15 provides that where the Secretary of State considers that there are grounds for giving a direction in respect of irresponsible prescribing (see iii above) and that 'the circumstances of the case require such a direction to be given with the minimum of delay' then a different procedure may be adopted and a six week temporary direction made, pending the resolution of the matter by a tribunal. (The period may be extended by 28 day periods provided the tribunal consents.) The temporary six week direction may not be made until the matter has been referred to a 'professional panel' (once again governed by Schedule 3) and until such a panel has reported that 'the information before it appears to it to afford reasonable grounds' for thinking that irresponsible prescribing has occurred.

The provision of Section 17 of the Misuse of Drugs Act should also be noted. This comes into play in the following circumstances:

'. . . if it appears to the Secretary of State that there exists in any area in Great Britain a social problem caused by the extensive misuse of dangerous or otherwise harmful drugs in that area . . .' then a notice may be served, inter alia, on any doctor practising in that area to 'require him to furnish to the Secretary of State, with respect to any such drugs specified in the notice and as regards any period so specified, such particulars as may be so specified relating to the quantities in which and the number and frequency of the occasions on which those drugs – (a) in the case of a doctor, were prescribed, administered or supplied by him; . . .'.

It should be noted that pharmacists on whom similar notice may also be served under this Section can be required amongst other things to give 'the names and addresses of doctors on whose prescriptions any dangerous or otherwise harmful drugs to which the notice relates were supplied'. It is a criminal offence to fail without reasonable excuse to give the required particulars or knowingly or recklessly to supply false information.

3.5 Notification of and Supply to Drug Addicts

The law concerning these issues is contained in the Misuse of Drugs (Notification of, and Supply to Addicts) Regulations (S.I. 1973 No.799) as amended.

3.5.1 Notification

Regulation 3 states that '. . . any doctor who attends a person who he considers, or has reasonable grounds to suspect, is addicted to any drug shall within 7 days of the attendance, furnish in writing to the Chief Medical Officer at the Home Office such of the following particulars with respect to that person as are known to the doctor, that is to say, the name, address, sex, date of birth and National Health Service number of that person, the date of the attendance and the name of the drug or drugs concerned'.

However, the doctor need not make such a notification if:

1   He 'is of the opinion, formed in good faith, that the continued administration of the drug or drugs concerned is required for the purpose of treating organic disease or injury; or'

2   If the required particulars have been supplied during the last 12 months by either

    (a) the doctor, or

    (b) where the doctor is a partner of or employed by a firm of general practitioners a partner or employed doctor in that firm, or

    (c) where the attendance is on behalf of another doctor (whether for payment, or not) by that other doctor or

    (d) if the attendance is at a hospital by a doctor on the staff of that hospital.

3.5.2 Supply

Regulation 4 states that a doctor shall not administer or supply (or authorise others to do so) to a person who the doctor considers or has reasonable grounds to suspect is addicted to any drugs (see below) the following substances: cocaine, diamorphine, or salts and any preparations or products containing same except:

    (a) for the purpose of treating organic disease or injury;

    (b) under and in accordance with a licence issued by the Secretary of State; or

    (c) under the authority of a doctor who has such a licence.

The term drug in both the above contexts is defined to mean the following controlled drugs listed in the Schedule below:

Cocaine	Methadone
Dextromoramide	Morphine
Diamorphine	Opium
Dipipanone	Oxycodone
Hydrocodone	Pethidine
Hydromorphone	Phenazocine
Levorphanol	Piritramide

Also included are the stereoisomeric forms of the above (but not dextrorphan) and ester or ether forms of the substances (but not one on Part II Schedule 2 of the Misuse of Drugs Act) and any salt or preparation or product containing same.

NB: Prescribing of controlled drugs of dependence otherwise than in the course of *bona fide* treatment could result in disciplinary proceedings. (See para 44 of GMC blue booklet.)

3.6   Possession and Supply of Medicinal Products

3.6.1   Introduction

It is not a criminal offence for a member of the public to possess a medicinal product but restrictions are placed upon the selling of same products. Section 7 of the Medicines Act 1968 prohibits persons acting in the course of business, ie commercially, from selling, supplying or manufacturing for sale any 'medicinal product' (see glossary for definition). Contravention of this provision is a criminal offence. There are various exemptions to this rule, some of which are dealt with below. Many of these relate to situations where a clinical trial is involved. There is one exemption which relates specifically to doctors (see below), and there are also provisions which relate to situations where a doctor has prescribed the medicinal product in question.

3.6.2   Supply of Medicinal Products for Use in a Clinical Trial

The provisions regarding clinical trials start off in Section 31(2) by prohibiting the commercial sale or supply (or acts leading to same) of any medicinal product for the purposes of a clinical trial. Contravention of this prohibition is a criminal offence. The Act then goes on to list a number of situations where a criminal offence would not in fact be committed and many of these exemptions relate to the involvement of doctors in the clinical trial in question. The Act defines the expression 'clinical trial' (see glossary).

3.6.2.1 Exemptions

1   Holding a product licence.

If a person holds a product licence 'which authorises the clinical trial in question' (or is acting under the instructions of the holder of same), and acts in accordance with the terms of the licence then the prohibition does not apply. (Section 31(3)(a).)

2   Existence of a clinical trial certificate.

If the certificate is in force and states that the licensing authority has consented to the clinical trial in question and the trial is to be carried out in accordance with that certificate then the prohibition does not apply. (Section 31(3)(b).)

3   Sale or supply by doctor.

If a doctor (a) sells, supplies (or procures the sale or supply) of a medicinal product; or (b) procures the manufacture or assembly of a medicinal product specially prepared to his order; or (c) if he is to be (or he is acting at the request of) the doctor (or dentist) by whom, or under whose direction, the product is to be administered then the prohibition does not apply. See Section 31(5) but also note the provisions of Section 31(6). This provides that the exemption provided by Section 31(5) is not applicable if the 'clinical trial in question is to be carried out under arrangements made by, or at the request of, a third party (that is to say, a person who is not the doctor or dentist, or one of the doctors or dentists, by whom, or under whose direction, one or more medicinal products are to be administered in that trial)'.

4   Sales in hospitals, pharmacies and health centres.

Section 31(7) states the prohibition does not apply to '. . . anything which is done in a registered pharmacy, a hospital or a health centre and is done there by or under the supervision of a pharmacist in accordance with a prescription given by a doctor or dentist; and those restrictions do not apply to anything done by or under the supervision of a pharmacist which consists of procuring the preparation or dispensing of a medicinal product in accordance with a prescription given by a doctor or dentist, or of procuring the assembly of a medicinal product'.

5   Manufacture of medicinal product to order of doctor.

The prohibition does not cover the commercial manufacture or assembly of a medicinal product if a doctor has stated '. . . that it is required for administration to a patient of his or is required, at the request of another doctor, or dentist, for administration to a patient of that other doctor or dentist'. Nor does it apply where done to the order of a pharmacist in accordance with a doctor's prescription. (Section 31(8).)

6   Notification to licensing authority of proposed trial.

The Medicines (Exemption from Licences) (Special Cases and Miscellaneous Provisions) Order 1972 (S.I. 1972 No.1200) as amended provides in Rule 4 that the prohibition will not apply if all the following conditions are satisfied:

(a)   The seller is selling the product exclusively for the purposes of use in a clinical trial (or to the extent that the product is to be used for some other purpose that use is authorised by a licence, certificate or other authority).

(b)   The clinical trial is not to be carried out under arrangements made by or on behalf of the manufacturer or person responsible for composition or the seller, unless such person is the doctor or dentist or one of same by whom or by whose direction the medicinal product is to be administered in that trial.

(c)   The doctor or dentist must notify the licensing authority of the proposed holding of the trial, specifying the product that is to be administered and the use of same and the name and address of the supplier.

(d) The licensing authority must not within 21 days (a longer period may be stipulated) have directed that this exemption is not to apply.

The Act provides that other exemptions may be stipulated by Order, eg The Medicines (Exemption from Licences) (Clinical Trials) Order 1974 (S.I. 1974 No.498) provides that certain products which might not strictly speaking be covered by a product licence, but only because of a change in manufacturing procedures or a difference in shape or lack of distinctive marks, can be exempted. Similarly exempted are products defined as being for control purposes only and licensed products surrounded by inert substances.

The Medicines (Exemption from Licences) (Clinical Trials) Order 1981 (S.I. 1981 No.164) additionally provides that the prohibition will not apply if certain conditions are observed. The conditions are set out in Article 4 of the Order and are as follows:

(a) 'the supplier has given or sent to the licensing authority a notice which states his intention to sell or supply, or procure the sale, supply, manufacture or assembly of medicinal products of the description in question for the purposes of a clinical trial and which is accompanied by

　　i　the particulars and summaries specified in Schedule 1 to this Order;

　　ii　A certificate signed by a doctor listing his medical and scientific qualifications who works within the UK and which states both that he is a medical adviser in the employment of, or consultant to, the supplier and that he has satisfied himself as to the accuracy of the summaries specified at paragraph 13 of Schedule 1 to this order and that, having regard to the contents of those summaries, he is of the opinion that it is reasonable for the proposed clinical trial to be undertaken.'

The 'summaries' in paragraph 13 are 'summaries of reports and evaluations of any experimental and biological studies and of other preclinical, clinical or laboratory studies carried out with each medicinal product, or its constituents, which in the view of the supplier are relevant to the assessment of the safety, quality or efficacy of the medicinal product together with references to relevant publications or other clinical trials.'

(b) The licensing authority must not have within a specific period (35 days from getting the notice although this can be extended by 28 days) have sent the supplier a notice stating that the exemption is not to apply.

(c) Lastly the supplier must give an undertaking to the licensing authority that he will inform them of:

'i any adverse reactions or effects associated with the administration of the medicinal product,

ii any other matter coming to his attention which might reasonably cause the licensing authority to think that the medicinal product could no longer be regarded as a product which could safely be administered for the purposes of the clinical trial or as a product which was of satisfactory quality for those purposes,

iii any change in respect of any of the matters specified in Schedule 2 to this order, and

iv any refusal to approve the clinical trial by a committee established or recognised by a health authority constituted under the National Health Service Act 1977 . . . or by the Medical Research Council . . .'

The exemption can last for up to three years if the stipulated conditions continue to be fulfilled unless the licensing authority terminates the right to take advantage of it.

NB: Schedules 1 and 2 of The Medicines (Exemption from Licences) Clinical Trials Order 1974 are not covered above in their entirety.

3.6.3 Supply of Medicinal Products by Doctors

Section 9 of the Medicines Act 1968 provides some exemption from the general prohibition in Section 7 for doctors, dentists and veterinary surgeons. In the case of doctors this means doctors who are registered medical practitioners.

Section 9 states that the restrictions in Section 7 (which prohibit commercial supply of medicinal products) do not apply to anything done by a doctor which:

'(a) relates to a medicinal product specifically prepared, or specially imported by him or to his order, for administration to a particular patient of his, and consists of manufacturing or assembling, or procuring the manufacture or assembly of, the product, or of selling or supplying, or procuring the sale or supply of, the product to that patient or to a person under whose care that patient is, or'

(b) when the doctor does likewise at the request of another doctor or dentist for administration to a patient of their own.

3.6.4 Prescribing Medicinal Products

Section 58(2)(a) of the Medicines Act 1968 provides that certain medicinal products may only be sold in accordance with a 'prescription given by an appropriate practitioner'.

The question of what products are covered, who is an 'appropriate practitioner' for these purposes and what must be contained in the prescription are dealt with in The Medicines (Products other than Veterinary Drugs) (Prescriptions

Only) Order 1983 (S.I. 1983 No.1212) as amended by The Medicines (Products other than Veterinary Drugs) (General Sales List) Order 1984 (S.I. 1984 No.756). The list of medicinal products controlled in this way is too long to reproduce here. It is contained in the Schedule to the Regulations and is amended from time to time. The phrase 'appropriate practitioner' includes doctors who are registered medical practitioners. The prescription must:

(a) be signed in ink with his own name by the practitioner giving it; and

(b) be written in ink or otherwise indelible (there is an exception for 'health', ie National Health Service prescriptions which are not for controlled drugs specified in Schedules to the Misuse of Drugs Regulations: these can be written by means of carbon paper or similar material and

(c) include the following particulars:
    i   the address of the practitioner
    ii the date
    iii the category of practitioner, eg registered medical practitioner
    iv in the case of doctors' prescriptions the name, address and age (if under 12) of the patient.

The prescription is not to be dispensed if it is more than six months old unless it is a repeat prescription in which case the first dispensing is not to take place more than six months after the date of the prescription. If a prescription does not specify how many times it is to be dispensed there can only be two dispensings of it except in the case of oral contraceptives which may be dispensed up to six times before the six months are up.

In an emergency, prescription only drugs which are not 'controlled' may be dispensed without a prescription if a doctor requests same and undertakes to supply a prescription within 72 hours.

3.6.5 Product Liability

The product liability provisions of Part I of the Consumer Protection Act 1987 came into force on 1 March 1988, implementing an EEC Directive, make producers of defective products strictly liable. The effect will be that if a person suffers damage as a result of a defective product, it will no longer be necessary to prove negligence, but only that the product was defective and the damage was as a result of the defective product. By virtue of the Act 'suppliers' will also become liable unless they can identify the 'producer', ie the manufacturer. Products for the purpose of the Act refers to goods, their raw materials and their component parts, including drugs, medical appliances and equipment. As potential suppliers of products there will be a considerable burden on doctors to keep accurate records identifying the sources of products, to avoid liability.

Doctors may become liable either by acting as a supplier, eg dispensing drugs, by giving patients or fitting appliances, or by undertaking treatment in the consulting room; or by becoming producers themselves, eg by modifying drugs or appliances, or mixing medicines before supplying them to the patient. By modifying the product the doctor himself could well become liable. Strict liability will also attach to anyone who presents himself as the producer, eg by putting 'own brand' labels on the product. Where hospital doctors within the NHS supply drugs or appliances the hospital authority will be the supplier. The hospital owners of private hospitals will almost certainly be the supplier where doctors practise in private hospitals, or the hospital authority where doctors undertake private practice within an NHS hospital. However, those doctors practising privately from their own consulting rooms should observe the general guidance in this and the following section. Both doctors and health authorities fall within the scope of the Act and must consequently be aware of the provisions affecting them.

The intention of the Act is to facilitate injured consumers obtaining a remedy against manufacturers of defective products by requiring proof only that the product was defective. A duty of care and breach of duty need not be established and thus the plaintiff does not have to attribute negligence to a specific person or persons. Responsibility falls primarily on the manufacturer as producer, but if he cannot be identified it will rest with any supplier who cannot identify someone further up the chain. As many doctors and health care personnel are the last link in the chain of supply of medicines from manufacturer to patient, particular care must be taken to record the sources of all suppliers of goods. Records relating to the origin of any drug supplied to a patient must be kept for an eleven year period.

According to Section 3 of the Act, a defect exists '. . . if the safety of the product is not such as persons generally are entitled to expect'. Safety is defined in the context of risk of death or personal injury as well as risk of damage to property. The Act takes into account what people should reasonably expect the producer to have considered when the product was marketed and will cover warnings stated and instructions issued by the producer at the time the product was supplied.

The Government has chosen to allow a substantial 'development risk' defence (sometimes called the 'state of the art' defence) which would mean producers, eg of drugs, could escape liability if they could prove that the state of scientific and technical knowledge was such that the existence of a defect could not be discovered. Liability under the Act ceases ten years after the product was supplied but plaintiffs must commence their actions within three years of the discovery of the defect, the damage and the party responsible. The right of a consumer to sue in contract is unaffected, and a victim of a defective product may still be able to bring an action in negligence if he wishes, irrespective of the Act.

3.6.5.1 General Practice

Advice for general practitioners from the BMA's General Medical Services Committee issued in May 1988, prepared following consultation with the

DHSS and legal advisers, is that doctors supplying medicines are unlikely to be at risk if they:

'(a) *Adhere strictly to the labelling regulations which apply to all dispensed medicines*

These regulations apply to all supplies of medicines including those given in an emergency or 'out of the bag'. They require the containers of all medicines prepared or dispensed by a doctor, or prepared or dispensed in accordance with a prescription given by a doctor, to be labelled with:

i   The name of the person to whom the medicinal product is to be administered;

ii   The name, address and telephone number of the supplying doctor (or chemist);

iii   The date the medicines are dispensed;

iv   The words 'keep out of reach of children' or words of similar meaning.

In addition, though at the doctor's discretion, if the doctor has prescribed the medicine, the label should also indicate the name of the product, directions for use and precautions relating to use of the product in question.

(b) *Ensure that every instance of supply is recorded in the patient's clinical record*

This includes medicines supplied in an emergency or 'out of the bag'.

i   Doctors supplying drugs in a proprietary form need only record the brand name of the drug supplied as this identifies the manufacturer.

ii   The generic name of a drug does not identify the manufacturer and doctors supplying generic products should record the name of the manufacturer or their own supplier.

iii   The recording of batch numbers for products other than those supplied in accordance with paragraph 8 of this note should not generally be required.

iv   Records should be made of the manufacturer or supplier of products [such as dressings, appliances and injections] which are supplied or loaned to patients without a label.

(c) *Keep accurate records (invoices, etc) of their source of supply of all products and retain them for a period of 11 years.'*

The guidance note states that where a patient is no longer registered with a general practitioner and records have been returned to the Family Practitioner

Committee, the latter will provide for the safekeeping. However, Family Practitioner Committees will not provide for the safekeeping of additional papers which deal only with product liability information.

It concludes:

'7   General practitioners who supply medicines should be aware that they may be considered to be the manufacturer of -

    i   medicines they make up and dispense themselves, ie extemporaneously dispensed medicines.

    ii   products which they dilute other than in accordance with the instructions on the data sheet.

– and in these cases particular care should be exercised in maintaining accurate records.

8   The medical defence bodies have indicated that if a member were sued under the legislation they would be indemnified in the usual way provided that the goods were supplied in connection with the doctor's professional practice. The defence bodies have advised their members to note on a patient's clinical record the dosage, batch number, manufacturer and supplier of any free drug samples which they give to patients.'

3.6.5.2   Health Authorities

Circular HN(88)3 (HN(FP)(88)5 on 'Procurement Product Liability' issued in March 1988 'draws attention to the main implications for health authorities of Part I of the Consumer Protection Act 1987 and offers guidance to help minimise NHS liability for defective products'.

On record keeping the circular states:

'It will be apparent from the above guidance that in most instances the capacity to avoid liability or defend an action brought under Part I of the Act will depend substantially on the maintenance of clear, accurate and comprehensive records relating to the procurement, use, modification and supply of products. And, since an obligation arising from liability is extinguished only after a period of 10 years and up to one year is allowed for the serving of a writ, such records should be retained for a period of 11 years. . . . The Department does, however, recognise that local circumstances may make it very difficult or impracticable to record in equal or sufficient detail all products/actions to link a potentially defective product with a potential claimant. If the introduction and maintenance of new or more sophisticated systems will add substantially to an authority's costs, or disrupt patient service, the authority may wish to make its own judgement in balancing the effects of additional record keeping against the likelihood of claims. In this respect authorities should note that any increase in costs arising from a tightening up of procedures to minimise the possibility of litigation, will need to be met by health authorities from existing resources.

The price of any affected product marketed for sale by the NHS should allow for recovery of an appropriate proportion of these costs. The general rule that the Crown bears its own risks precludes the option of insurance cover against the increased risk of claims for damages. The cost of successful claims would be a direct health authority liability.'

On medicinal products the guidance states:

'It is recognised that particular problems may arise from the supply of medicinal preparations by hospital pharmacies as a result of the sheer volume of transactions and the extended chain by which a medicine can pass from producer to patient. In addition hospital pharmacies which make up preparations from ingredients will be regarded as producers for purposes of the Act. Liability for a defective product arising from the functions of a hospital pharmacy would, however, rest with the health authority and not the member of staff concerned. This liability could of course be avoided if the authority was not the producer within the meaning of the Act and either the authority's own supplier or the producer could be identified. This would require records to be kept along the lines indicated in paragraph 3. No detailed central guidance can be given to provide traceability of medicines along the supply chain but Regional Pharmaceutical Officers should consider the extent to which existing record keeping needs to be altered to meet the essential requirements of a system to link unambiguously the producer of the product, or its ingredients, with the end user. . . .'

In conclusion, the circular points out that while the guidance relates principally to medical supplies 'very few products are excluded from the provisions of the Act and authorities should recognise that they may be affected as suppliers, keepers and producers of non-medical items which may give rise to claims'. It advises that authorities should 'view the potential implications against the background of their existing liability in tort in the event of claims for damages'.

3.7 Import and Export of Drugs

So far as this country is concerned the legal controls over import and export of drugs depend on whether the substance in question is classified as a 'medicinal product' under the Medicines Act 1968 or as a 'controlled drug' under the Misuse of Drugs Act 1971. Doctors are given special exemptions when it comes to the import and export of medicinal products but the same does not apply where controlled drugs are concerned.

3.7.1 Medicinal Products

The Medicines Act 1968 provides in Section 7(2) that 'medicinal products' (see glossary) must not be exported in the course of business unless a 'product licence' is first obtained. Section 7(3) prohibits the importation of medicinal products except in accordance with a product licence. Breach of this Section is a criminal offence. To these general rules there are various exceptions.

See subchapters 3.6.2 and 3.6.3 for the special exemption for doctors, dentists and veterinary surgeons set out in Section 9 of the Act.

3.7.2   Clinical Trials

The general prohibition contained in Section 7 is also subject to some exceptions which relate to the importation of medicinal products for use in clinical trials.

Section 31(4) sets out the general position, which is that the importation of medicinal products for use in clinical trials is forbidden but there are exceptions to this in respect of persons holding product licences or clinical trial certificates and, under Section 31(5), in certain circumstances doctors and dentists.

The exemption for product licence holders is as follows: Section 31(4) states after setting out the general position that this restriction does not apply to someone who holds a product licence authorising such clinical trials and imports a product in accordance with that licence or imports a product to the order of a person who holds such a licence.

If a clinical trial certificate has been issued the prohibition against importation does not apply. This is provided the licensing authority has consented to the clinical trial in question, the certificate is in force and the trial is to be carried out in accordance with the licence. See Section 35(1).

The exemption for doctors and dentists is set out in Section 31(5). This states that Section 31(4) does not apply to a doctor or dentist '. . . specially importing a medicinal product, where (in any such case) he is, or acts at the request of, the doctor or dentist by whom, or under whose direction, the product is to be administered'.

NB This is also subject to the provisions of Section 31(6) – see subchapter 3.6.2.1.

3.8   Medicinal Tests on Animals

(The term 'medicinal tests on animals' is defined in Section 32(6) which is fully set out in the subchapter 7.3.1 Animal Experiments.)

Section 32(2) sets out the general position which is that the importation of medicinal products for the purposes of medicinal tests on animals is forbidden but there are exceptions to this if a product licence has been obtained or an animal test certificate has been issued. (See glossary.) The criteria by which product licences in this context and animal test certificates are considered valid for these purposes are similarly expressed as for product licences and clinical trial certificates respectively as set out above. (See subchapter 7.3.1 for the exact text.) Section 32 may also be modified by an order made under Section 35(8).

It should be noted that all the exceptions are subject to the fact that the Government has the power to prohibit the importation of certain medicinal products. This is stated in Section 62 pursuant to which for instance the following orders have been made:

The Medicines (Phenacetin Prohibition) Order 1979 (S.I. 1979 No.1181) and the Medicines (Bal Jivan Chamcho Prohibition) (No.2) Order 1979 (S.I. 1979 No.670).

Conversely Section 15 provides that the Government may order that exemptions to the general prohibitions in Section 7 also be made. Numerous orders have been made.

Also, under Section 13, any person may import without a licence a medicinal product for administration to himself or any other member of his household. Also permitted under this Section is the importation of a medicinal product specially imported by or to the order of a doctor (or dentist) for administration to a particular patient of his.

There are various other exemptions in the Act, but there is not space to detail them all.

3.9 Controlled Drugs

Section 3 of the Misuse of Drugs Act 1971 prohibits the import and export of controlled drugs (see glossary as to which drugs are controlled). Anyone who contravenes this provision could be prosecuted under legislation relating to Customs and Excise. A person would not be prosecuted, however, if he was exempted by any Regulation passed by virtue of Section 7 of the Act. Doctors as such are not exempted from the provisions. The Misuse of Drugs Regulations (S.I. 1985 No.2066) provide that Section 3 does not apply to controlled drugs listed in Schedules 4 and 5 to those Regulations. This exemption applies to everyone, not just doctors.

Also exempted from prosecution would be those who had obtained a licence to import and export controlled drugs and who acted in accordance with same.

It follows from the above that anyone wishing to take a controlled drug out of the country must apply for a licence before doing so. This applies, for example, to general practitioners wishing to take emergency supplies out of the country, as well as to individuals currently receiving a controlled drug on prescription (but see below). In order to consider licence applications from individuals, written confirmation is required from the prescribing doctor of the name, form, strength and quality of drug(s) involved. Applications should be made at least two weeks before departure date and the days of departure and return must be stated. Anyone who wishes to apply for such a licence should apply to the Drugs Branch of the Home Office, Queen Anne's Gate, London SW1H 9AT. Special arrangements exist for doctors wishing to accompany groups of pilgrims to Lourdes in the capacity of Medical Officer. A standard form, number MD 50 A, is available on request from the Home Office on which such doctors may apply for the necessary licence and these arrangements have been approved by the French authorities.

The Home Office is not prepared to issue licences to doctors who wish to take controlled drugs abroad solely in case an emergency may arise. However, sympathetic consideration would be given to applications from doctors who were, for example, accompanying hazardous expeditions.

It must be noted that both doctors and patients wishing to take drugs abroad must comply not just with the laws of this country but also with the law of the country to which they wish to take the substance in question. The Home Office will expect the person applying for the export licence to have first obtained an import licence from the country to which it is wished to take the drugs.

3

The licence authorises the holder to carry the controlled drugs specified on the licence out of the UK under the conditions stated on the licence and to bring back any residue.

An 'Open General Licence' (OGL) for the import/export of small quantities of drugs was introduced on 1 March 1987. It provides a general authority for: an ordinary traveller carrying controlled drugs for medical reasons, either for himself or for a member of his household who is unable to administer the drug himself; or a doctor accompanying a patient who requires treatment during a journey from and/or to the UK. A Schedule sets out the controlled drugs and the maximum quantity allowed.

Such a licence does not apply '(a) to any controlled drug which is not contained in a medicinal product within the meaning of the Medicines Act 1968; (b) unless the controlled drug is under the direct personal supervision of the personal importing or exporting it; (c) to the exportation of any controlled drug by a person who is not lawfully in possession of the drug.' (See glossary for definition of medicinal product.)

It should be noted that as in the case of individual licences the OGL does not have any standing outside the UK. Travellers should always obtain clearance from the representatives of the country of destination in the UK, ie embassy or consulate, for the import of the drug into that country prior to departure from the UK.

4 Medical Practices

Doctors may practise medicine alone, or in partnership with others, and medical practices may take on National Health Service work or private work, or both. A number of legal implications arise as a result of this business activity. We deal with the following:

To what extent, if any, may the existence of the practice or the attributes of the doctors be advertised?

Is it legal for a doctor to sell the goodwill of his practice?

May partners in a medical practice bind each other to an agreement that if one of them leaves that person will not set up a rival practice nearby? (The legal expression for this is a 'restrictive covenant'.)

What legal obligations is the doctor under to members of the public and to his staff?

4.1 Advertising

Certain types of advertising in relation to medical treatment would contravene the criminal law. For instance, no person is allowed to advertise treatments for cancer. See Cancer Act 1939 which provides in Section 4:

'No person shall take part in the publication of any advertisement:

(a) containing an offer to treat any person for cancer, or to prescribe any remedy therefor, or to give any advice in connection with the treatment thereof.'

It is not, however, a criminal offence in this context to advertise so far as is reasonably necessary to bring the article in question to the notice of registered medical practitioners, nurses and pharmacists etc, or if the advertisement is published only in a technical journal circulated within the medical profession.

Secondly, the Venereal Disease Act 1917 provides in Section 2(1) 'a person shall not by any advertisement or any public notice or announcement treat or offer to treat any person for venereal disease, or prescribe or offer to prescribe any remedy therefor, or offer to give or give any advice in connection with the treatment thereof'.

This restriction does not apply to any advertisement by a local or public authority, published with the sanction of the Secretary of State, or in any publication sent only to duly qualified medical practitioners, or wholesale or retail chemists for the purposes of their business.

There are also restrictions against the advertisement of medicinal products if those advertisements are likely to lead to their use, except under the instruction of a doctor or a dentist.

The GMC make it quite clear in their April 1987 blue booklet (paras 58-60) that self-promotion, canvassing and disparagement of professional colleagues amount to serious professional misconduct.

In paragraphs 93-96 the GMC consider the circumstances in which questions of self-promotion most commonly arise, namely notices or announcements, questions of self-promotion arising from relationships between doctors and organisations providing clinical, diagnostic or medical advisory services, public references to doctors by other companies or other organisations, and self-promotion arising from articles in books, broadcasting or television appearances by doctors, or signposts or notice boards relating to health centres or medical centres, or choice of titles for such centres or for group practices.

The BMA in their *Handbook of Medical Ethics* (paras 8.9–8.20) deal with the issue of what sorts of conduct would be interpreted as being contrary to the rules against advertising.

The provision of 'in-house' practice leaflets by general practices and partnerships does not constitute advertising provided the information included on services provided is accurate, non-promotional and factual. It should not draw attention to the achievements, educational or otherwise, of the doctors of the practice as a whole.

4.2 Sale of Goodwill

Statute provides in effect that it is a criminal offence to buy or sell the goodwill of a National Health Service (NHS) practice. The relevant legislation is contained in the National Health Service Act 1977 (as amended) (England and Wales only) and the National Health Service (Scotland) Act 1978. Certain dispositions would be deemed for these purposes to constitute the sale of goodwill, but doctors who are in doubt as to whether any particular transaction could amount to a sale of goodwill may clarify the position with the Medical Practices Committee, and thus may have a good defence to any prosecution later brought. Details of the provisions are as follows.

Section 54 of the English Statute and Section 35 of the Scottish Statute provide that where the name of any medical practitioner is or has been at any time entered on any list of medical practitioners undertaking to provide general medical services, it shall be unlawful subsequently to sell the goodwill or any part of the goodwill of the medical practice of that medical practitioner.

However, there are two situations where this general prohibition does not apply.

'Where a medical practitioner whose name has ceased to be entered on any list of medical practitioners undertaking to provide general medical services practises in the locality of a Family Practitioner Committee without his name ever having been entered on a list of medical practitioners undertaking to provide general medical services' then the sale of the goodwill of his practice (or any part of it) in that locality is not unlawful. Such a sale would also not be unlawful if the sale is by a medical practitioner 'whose name has never been entered on a list of medical practitioners undertaking to provide general medical services there, notwithstanding that any part of the goodwill to be sold is attributable to such a practice previously carried on by a person whose name was entered on such a list'.

In this context 'general medical services' is defined as services provided pursuant to the provisions of part II of the National Health Service Act 1977 by arrangement with the Family Practitioner Committee.

Schedule 10 of the English Statute and Schedule 9 of the Scottish Statute provide that anyone who buys or sells the goodwill of a medical practice in contravention of the above provisions is guilty of a criminal offence, although in England and Wales no such prosecution can take place without the consent of the Director of Public Prosecutions.

4

In case there should be any attempt to avoid these provisions by disguising the sale of goodwill the Schedules set out circumstances in which a sale of goodwill will be deemed to have taken place.

For example, disposing of the premises will be assumed to be the sale of goodwill if the price is 'substantially in excess of the consideration which might reasonably have been expected if the premises had not previously been used for the purposes of medical practice'.

Similarly, if in pursuance of a partnership agreement a partner pays a 'valuable consideration' (ie anything of value, not just money) to enter a partnership or is given the same to leave it then this too may be assumed to amount to the sale of goodwill. The same assumption may be made if an assistant works for a cheap rate and is later accepted into the partnership or if a person agrees for a valuable consideration to do or not to do anything to facilitate his entry to the partnership, or if the person pays such a consideration for such entry.

It might be difficult for doctors to know when any particular transaction might land them in the criminal courts. Therefore, the Schedules provide that any medical practitioner or his personal representative may apply to the Medical Practices Committee for the latter's opinion as to whether a proposed transaction would involve the unlawful sale of goodwill. The committee must consider any such application and, if satisfied that the transaction would not have such an effect, they must issue a certificate to that effect. The certificate must set out 'all the material circumstances disclosed to the committee'. Production of such a certificate will provide a good defence to any subsequent criminal proceedings unless it becomes obvious that there was a failure to disclose a relevant factor.

Apart from the statutory prohibition referred to above, there is no law against the sale of medical goodwill. Private practitioners should be careful, however, before selling their goodwill, to ensure that they are not breaking the law by virtue of the present or past appearance of their name on the list of practitioners willing to provide general medical services.

It is also worth noting that para 64 of the April 1987 GMC blue booklet makes it clear that improper arrangements to extend a doctor's practice may amount to serious professional misconduct.

4.3   Restrictive Covenants

It is common for partnership deeds to provide that if a partner leaves he may not set up a rival business nearby. There has been much litigation on this subject occurring when partners seek to enforce such a provision against an ex-partner. The latter may argue that the provision should not be enforced. In the case of private medical practice as with other businesses such a restriction to be enforceable must go no further than is reasonable for the protection of the goodwill.

At one time such agreements were not considered to be enforceable in the case of NHS practices. However, in the case of Kerr v Morris [1986] 3 AER 217 the court decided that a restrictive covenant could be enforced against a doctor quitting an NHS partnership.

The question of whether or not a particular restrictive covenant in a partnership agreement is or is not reasonable is a matter for the particular circumstances of each case. Factors such as the geographical breadth of the restriction must be considered as well as the general public interest when weighed against the interests of the parties. A partnership agreement normally also regulates the financial arrangements between the partners and in the case of a medical practice may have to cater for matters such as the use and ownership of the surgery. In general it is advisable that all partners take legal/accountancy advice when drawing up or entering into a partnership agreement.

4.4   Responsibilities Imposed by the Occupiers' Liability Act

If a member of the public suffered an accident whilst on the doctor's premises could the doctor be sued for damages?

The Occupiers' Liability Acts 1957 and 1984 (not applicable in Scotland and Northern Ireland) stipulate what responsibilities are owed to members of the public by occupiers of premises.

First it is necessary to consider what is meant by the term 'occupier'. This is not defined in the Acts and so the original common law rules still apply. Halsbury's Laws Volume 34, paragraph 19 states: 'in order to be an occupier exclusive occupation is not required, and the test is whether a person has some degree of control associated with, and arising from, his presence in, and use of, or activity in, the premises'. It follows that doctors who are partners in a medical practice would be regarded as occupiers of the premises where the practice was situate for the purposes of being responsible under this legislation.

The responsibility owed depends on whether the member of the public in question was on the one hand invited or permitted to be on the premises by the doctors, eg a patient, or had not been so invited or permitted, eg a trespasser or someone such as a drug company representative who had just walked in the door unannounced in the hope of selling something to the partnership.

Responsibility for the first category of persons, referred to as visitors from now on, is dealt with in the Occupiers' Liability Act 1957. A 'duty of care' is owed to all visitors and is defined in Section 2(2) as follows:

'The common duty of care is a duty to take such care as in all the circumstances of the case is reasonable to see that the visitor will be reasonably safe in using the premises for the purposes for which he is invited or permitted by the occupier to be there.'

4

In this context the Act states that an occupier must be prepared for children to be less careful than adults. The Act anticipates and does not forbid the contracting out by the occupier of his responsibilities by eg a disclaimer notice, but a later piece of legislation, the Unfair Contract Terms Act 1977, puts considerable limits on the extent to which businesses may evade their obligations to visitors to their premises by such methods. That Act states in Section 2(1):

'A person cannot by reference to any contract term or to a notice given to persons generally or to particular persons exclude or restrict his liability for death or personal injury resulting from negligence.'

The above only deals with liability for death or injury responsibility for which the occupier cannot avoid. The Act goes on to state that liability for other loss or damage, eg damage to property, can only be contracted out of if the term or notice in question is reasonable. (The Act gives guidance on that point in a later section.) Section 2(4)(a) of the Occupiers' Liability Act also states that even if the occupier warns of the existence of the danger this does not necessarily absolve him of all responsibility unless in all the circumstances the warning 'was enough to enable the visitor to be reasonably safe'.

Section 2(5) of the Occupiers' Liability Act does state, however, that the occupier is under no obligation to a visitor in respect of risks willingly accepted by that visitor.

There are special provisions in respect of 'independent contractors' on the premises, eg builders, plumbers etc. The Act states (Section 2(3)(b)) that an occupier is entitled to expect that a person in the exercise of his calling will appreciate and guard against any special risks ordinarily incidental to it (so far as the occupier leaves him free to do so). In the case of Roles v Nathan, Roles v Carney [1963] 2 AER 908 CA two chimney sweeps were killed by carbon monoxide fumes while sealing up a sweephole. Evidence was given to the effect that they had been warned of the danger on numerous occasions by an expert employed by the occupier. It was held that the occupier was not responsible for their deaths. Not only had sufficient warning been given for purposes of Section 2(4)(a) (see above) but the danger was a special risk ordinarily incident to the exercise of their calling against which the occupier might expect them to guard. Section 2(4) (b) of the Act also stipulates that if the visitor is damaged as a result of faulty work done by an independent contractor then the occupier is not to be automatically liable for what occurred, provided, that is, that the occupier acted reasonably in entrusting the work to the contractor by taking reasonable steps to satisfy himself that the contractor was competent to perform it and that the work had been done properly.

4

Following the passing of the Occupiers' Liability Act 1957 there were a number of cases concerning the responsibility of occupiers to persons other than visitors, eg children straying on to railway lines. This led to the passing of the Occupiers' Liability Act 1984 which codifies the law on this question. First it should be noted that the 1984 Act does not impose any liability for loss of or damage to property. The duty is firstly owed in respect of any risk of a person other than a visitor suffering injury on the premises by reason of any damage due to the state of the premises or to things done or omitted to be done on them. The occupier is, however, still only liable for any injury suffered by persons other than his visitors if a number of criteria apply:

1   if the occupier is aware of the danger or has reasonable grounds to believe that it exists, and

2   if he knows or has reasonable grounds to believe that the person is in the vicinity of the danger concerned or that he may come into the vicinity of the danger, and

3   if the risk is one against which in all the circumstances of the case he may reasonably be expected to offer the other some protection.

If all the above exist then there is a duty of care, and the extent of it is to take such care as is reasonable in all the circumstances to see that a person other than a visitor does not suffer injury on the premises by reason of the danger concerned. The occupier may absolve himself from the duty by taking such steps as are reasonable in all the circumstances to give warning of the danger concerned or to discourage persons from incurring the risk. Note too that if the person willingly accepts the risk in question no duty is owed then by virtue of the Act.

It is obvious from what is said above that it is highly desirable to be insured against any claim under the Occupiers' Liability legislation.

4.5 Responsibilities Imposed by the Health and Safety at Work etc. Act 1974

The legislation above which relates to occupiers' liability provides that members of the public who suffer an accident on premises may be able to sue the person in control of those premises for damages in the civil courts. The Health and Safety at Work etc. Act 1974 additionally imposes obligations on employers, the self-employed, business occupiers and workers, breach of which could result in criminal prosecution. Doctors, therefore, who employ others or are self-employed or who are employed should take note of these provisions. An amendment to the Act in 1987 removed Crown immunity from National Health Service premises.

The aims of the Act are stated to be, amongst other things, to secure the health, safety and welfare of persons at work and to protect members of the public from risks that might be created by the work activities of others. In this context the meaning of work has been extended to include any activity involving genetic manipulation (Health and Safety (Genetic Manipulation) Regulation (S.I. 1978 No.752)) or the keeping or handling of certain pathogens (Health and Safety (Dangerous Pathogens) Regulations (S.I. 1981 No.1011)). The Act sets out a number of statutory duties owed by various persons to various categories of people and although, as stated, a breach of these obligations could result in a criminal prosecution the Act states that breach of any of them does not of itself confer a right on the aggrieved person to sue in the civil courts.

Section 2 of the Act sets out what general duties are owed by employers to their employees as follows:

'It shall be the duty of every employer to ensure, so far as is reasonably practicable, the health, safety and welfare at work of all his employees. This duty is stated to include in particular: .

(a) the provision and maintenance of plant and systems of work that are, so far as is reasonably practicable, safe and without risks to health;

(b) arrangements for ensuring, so far as is reasonably practicable, safety and absence of risks to health in connection with the use, handling, storage and transport of articles and substances;

(c) the provision of such information, instruction, training and supervision as is necessary to ensure, so far as is reasonably practicable, the health and safety at work of his employees;

(d) so far as is reasonably practicable as regards any place of work under the employer's control, the maintenance of it in a condition that is safe and without risks to health and the provision and maintenance of means of access to and egress from it that are safe and without such risks;

(e) the provision and maintenance of a working environment for his employees that is, so far as is reasonably practicable, safe without risks

55

to health and adequate as regards facilities and arrangements for their welfare at work.'

Except in 'prescribed' cases (one of which is employers who employ fewer than five persons) each employer must prepare a written statement of his general policy regarding the health and safety at work of his employees and the organisation and arrangements for the time being in force for carrying out that policy. This statement has to be brought to the notice of all employees.

Employers must also note the provision of the Employers' Liability (Compulsory Insurance) Act 1969 (not applicable in Northern Ireland). This provides that every employer carrying on any business (later defined to include a profession) in Great Britain must insure and maintain insurance under an approved policy and with an authorised insurer 'against liability for bodily injury or disease sustained by his employees, and arising out of and in the course of their employment in Great Britain in that business'. Failure to insure as above is a criminal offence. There is no obligation to insure against injuries or diseases suffered or contracted outside Great Britain. Also Section 2 lists various relatives who do not need to be covered. The certificate of insurance must be displayed and the Employers' Liability (Compulsory Insurance) General Regulations (S.I. 1971 No.11/17) prohibit the inclusion of certain conditions in the insurance policy and fix the amount of cover required.

Section 3 of the Health and Safety at Work etc. Act 1974 sets out the general duties owed by employers and self-employed persons to members of the public other than their employees. The duty owed in both cases is to conduct their undertakings in such a way as to ensure, so far as is reasonably practicable, that persons not in their employment who may be affected thereby are not thereby exposed to risks to their health and safety.

Section 4 deals with the duties owed by persons concerned with premises (ie each person who has, to any extent, control of the premises) to persons who are not their employees but who 'use non-domestic premises made available to them as a place of work or as a place where they may use plant or substances provided for their use there'. The duty owed is 'to take such measures as it is reasonable for a person in his position to take to ensure, so far as is reasonably practicable, that the premises, all means of access thereto or egress therefrom available for use by persons using the premises, and any plant or substance in the premises or, as the case may be, provided for use there, is or are safe and without risks to health'.

The duties owed by employees are set out in Section 7: 'it shall be the duty of every employee while at work

(a) to take reasonable care for the health and safety of himself and other persons who may be affected by his acts or omissions at work; and

(b) as regards any duty or requirement imposed on his employer or any other person by or under any of the relevant statutory provisions, to co-operate with him so far as is necessary to enable that duty or requirement to be performed or complied with.'

It is a criminal offence to fail to discharge any of the above duties.

It is also a criminal offence to disregard any provision laid down in Regulations made under the Act.

One such set of Regulations is the Reporting of Injuries, Diseases and Dangerous Occurrences Regulations (S.I. 1985 No.2023). These provide for the compulsory reporting of certain mishaps at work to the enforcing authority. The following must be reported. Any death resulting from an accident at work. Any injury or 'condition' arising as above, the categories of same being listed. They include various fractures, amputations, eye injuries, burns, loss of consciousness from lack of oxygen and 'either acute illness requiring medical treatment, or loss of consciousness, resulting in either case from absorption of any substance by inhalation, ingestion or through the skin'. Also 'acute illness requiring medical treatment where there is reason to believe that this resulted from exposure to a pathogen or infected material; and any other injury which results in . . .' immediate hospital admission for more than 24 hours.

There is also a duty to report the fact that a person has been incapacitated for more than three consecutive days as a result of an accident at work, and if an employee has suffered from a reportable condition and then dies from it within one year that death must be reported. If a person at work suffers from one of the diseases listed in the Schedule to the Regulations then if he has been engaged in the activity listed opposite that disease that fact must be reported if a medical diagnosis of the condition has been made.

Certain dangerous occurrences must also be reported. These too are listed in Article 10. The obligations above do not apply 'to a patient when undergoing treatment in a hospital or in the surgery of a doctor or dentist'.

The relevant medical authority under the Health and Safety at Work etc. Act 1974 is the Employment Medical Advisory Service (EMAS).

4.6 Responsibilities Imposed on Employers

Doctors in general practice will probably be employing others. In their position as employers those doctors should be aware that employed persons have a considerable number of rights, violation of which could lead to an award against the employer in the industrial tribunal or in the civil courts. Doctors who are themselves employed might be interested to know what rights they in turn have. Employment law is a huge subject and all that can be done here is to give a very brief outline only of the provisions. A comprehensive guide to the subject is Ellis N, *Employing Staff*, 2nd Edition, London: BMJ, 1987.

It is necessary to consider briefly what is meant by employment. The obligations discussed below are only owed by doctor employers to their employees or 'servants' and not to 'independent contractors', eg a plumber called in to do one job on the partnership premises. In most cases the distinction between the two will be obvious. There is much case law on the more borderline situations but such debates are out of the scope of this book.

In the following paragraphs the rights available to all employees are dealt with, followed by the special provisions for women and ethnic minorities.

The following rights are all contained in the Employment Protection (Consolidation) Act 1978 (not applicable in Northern Ireland).

4.6.1 Right to Have Particulars of Terms of Employment

Sections 1–6 of the Act deal with this subject. Within 13 weeks of starting their job employees are entitled to receive from their employer a written statement with various details including a recital of who is employing whom and the date the employment began, hours of work, holidays, sick pay, pensions, length of notice either side, job title, disciplinary procedures.

4.6.2 Right to Have Itemised Pay Statement

Section 8 states this must include gross wage, details of all deductions and net wage.

4.6.3 Rights Relating to Trade Union Membership

Section 23 forbids victimisation (as opposed to dismissal: see later) of any employee in relation to his joining or taking a part in trade union activities or in relation to his not joining a trade union.

4.6.4 Rights to Have Time Off Work

Sections 27 and 28 set out what rights employees have to have time off work in relation to trade union activities. Section 29 states that employees must be given time off (there being no statutory right to be paid whilst not at work) to perform various public duties. The duties in question are:

Justice of the Peace (JP).

Member of a statutory tribunal.

Member of a Regional Health Authority, Family Practitioner Committee, Health Board etc.

Member of governing body of school or water authority.

The time that must be allowed must be reasonable, regard being had particularly to certain listed criteria.

If an employee has been given notice by reason of redundancy then he must be given time off to look for work or make arrangements for training (Section 31).

4.6.5 Rights to Have Minimum Periods of Notice

The employer and employee can agree to lengthen the period of notice but the periods below represent the minimum which must be given. If the employee has been employed for a month or more the employee must give at least one week's notice and the employer the following. If the employee has been employed for less than two years: one week. If the employee has been employed for more than two years but not less than 12 years: one week per year employed. If the employee has been employed for 12 years or more not less than 12 weeks. (Section 49.)

4.6.6 Right to Have Written Statement of Reasons for Dismissal

If the employee's employment is terminated with or without notice or if a fixed term of employment ends and is not renewed (certain fixed term contracts are not covered at all by the Act if the employee agrees that the Act should not apply) then the employee may demand that the employer give a written statement of the reasons within 14 days. This does not apply however if the employment has not lasted for as long as six months. (Section 53.)

4.6.7 Right Not to be Unfairly Dismissed

These provisions apply only if the employee has been employed continuously for two years and has not reached retirement age (except when dismissal relates to trade union activities). Dismissal can be deemed to take place not only where the employer ends the employment with or without notice, but also when the employee walks out in circumstances where the employer's behaviour is held to justify his doing so without notice (referred to as 'constructive dismissal'). Section 57 attempts to define the meaning of 'unfair'. It is for the employer to show the reason for the dismissal and that that reason either falls within the listed categories below or amounts to some other substantial reason in either case justifying dismissal. The listed reasons are those:

(a) related to the capability or qualifications of the employee for performing work of the kind which he was employed by the employer to do, or

(b) related to the conduct of the employee, or

(c) that the employee was redundant, or

(d) that the continuation of the employment would be unlawful.

Also the issue of whether the dismissal was fair or unfair depends on whether the employer acted reasonably or unreasonably in treating the incident as sufficient reason for dismissing the employee and that question is to be determined in accordance with equity and the substantial merits of the case.

An employee has three months in which to complain to an industrial tribunal about unfair dismissal and the tribunal, if satisfied the dismissal was indeed unfair, may either make an award of damages or order reinstatement.

4.6.8   Right to Redundancy Payments

An employee who has been continuously employed for two years and is dismissed for redundancy is entitled to a redundancy payment. The Act lays down the criteria for calculating the amount.

4.6.9   Rights to Statutory Sick Pay

This is dealt with by the Social Security and Housing Benefits Act 1982 (as amended), which provides that employers must pay sick pay to their employees in certain circumstances (a refund being claimable via National Insurance contributions). The employee cannot claim any sick pay for the first three days off sick but thereafter is entitled to claim same at a stated rate up to the equivalent of 28 weeks' pay in any period of up to three years. Thereafter the employee must claim the benefit from the state. The employee need not obtain a medical certificate in the first week but must obtain one thereafter.

4.6.10   The Right to Time Off for Antenatal Care

Section 31A of the Employment Protection (Consolidation) Act 1978 provides that a pregnant woman is entitled to time off work for antenatal care if advised to go for same by a registered medical practitioner, registered health visitor or midwife. The employer still must pay the woman but can demand a certificate confirming the pregnancy.

4.6.11   The Right to Return to Work After Having a Child

This is set out in Section 33 of the Employment Protection (Consolidation) Act 1978. The conditions are as follows. The woman must have been employed before the beginning of the 11th week before the expected week of confinement. The woman must then have been continuously employed for two years by the employer. The woman must give the employer 21 days' written notice of her intention to be absent on grounds of pregnancy (or the notice must be given as soon as is reasonably practicable) and that she intends to return to work for the employer and the expected week of the confinement.

Forty nine days or more after the expected week of confinement the employer can ask for written confirmation that the woman still wants to return. She must answer within 14 days (or as soon as is reasonably practicable).

The right is to return before the end of the 29th week after the week of confinement to work for the employer (or his successor) on terms and conditions no less favourable or if this is not practicable the employer may offer suitable alternative employment and if the woman is redundant he must offer a suitable vacancy if there is one.

If the employer refuses to take the woman back this can be treated as unfair dismissal with the resulting consequences (see above) unless when the woman left the total number of employees did not exceed five and it is not reasonably practicable to permit her to return.

Section 60 also states that in certain circumstances a dismissal on the grounds of pregnancy will be assumed to be unfair.

4.6.12 Right to Statutory Maternity Pay

This right is set out in the Social Security Act 1986. As with statutory sick pay the responsibility of paying is imposed on the employer, who can claim reimbursement from the State. The payments must begin not earlier than 11 weeks before the expected week of confinement and be for a maximum of 18 weeks. The woman must have been employed by the employer for at least 26 weeks.

4.6.13 The Right Not to be Discriminated Against

The Equal Pay Act 1970 (not applicable in Northern Ireland) implies an 'equality' clause in every woman's contract of employment. This ensures that if a woman is employed on similar work to a man she must not be employed on less favourable terms or be excluded from any benefits.

The Sex Discrimination Act 1975 also makes discrimination in the field of employment unlawful, ie there must be no discrimination in the arrangements for who should be offered employment or in the terms on which employment is offered. Refusing or deliberately omitting to offer employment on grounds of sex is also unlawful. If a woman is employed it is unlawful to discriminate against her in respect of opportunities for promotion, transfer or training or any other facility or service.

Partnerships should also note that where there is a partnership of six or more it is unlawful to discriminate against prospective or existing partners.

By virtue of the Race Relations Act 1976 race discrimination too is unlawful, the provisions being similar to those for sexual discrimination.

4

5 Specialised Areas of Medicine

5.1 Ships' Doctors

Legislation provides that certain appointments on board ship are only to be held by registered medical practitioners and some British registered ships must carry registered medical practitioners on board. There are also provisions for the medical examination of seamen, for the giving of medical treatment in circumstances where no qualified doctor is on board and for the carrying of medical supplies etc in ships. The duty of confidentiality owed by ships' doctors to seamen should also be considered.

Section 47 of the Medical Act 1983 provides that no person who is not a fully registered medical practitioner (subchapter 9.1 for definition) shall hold any appointment as physician, surgeon or other medical officer in, *inter alia*, the naval, military or air service. Previous legislation which has now been repealed used to extend this provision to appointments in any emigrant or other vessel. However, Section 43(1) of the Merchant Shipping Act 1970 gave the Board of Trade power to make Regulations requiring certain ships to carry such number of qualified doctors as might be specified. The Merchant Shipping (Ship's Doctors) Regulations (S.I. 1981 No.1065) made under this section provide the following: every UK ship which goes to sea having 100 or more persons on board must carry a qualified doctor. Qualified in this context means a fully registered medical practitioner. This provision does not, however, apply to ships going solely between places within the Near Continental Trading area and the Secretary of State does have power to grant specific or general exemptions to this provision.

The Merchant Shipping (Medical Examination) Regulations (S.I. 1983 No.808) provide that in sea-going ships of 1,600 gross register tonnage or over, a seafarer must not be employed unless he holds a valid medical fitness certificate. Each applicant must be examined by an approved medical practitioner (ie approved for the purpose by the Secretary of State). If the practitioner considers that the applicant is fit he must issue him with a medical fitness certificate which may be restricted as to capacity or sea service or geographical areas.

If there is no doctor on board then Section 25 of the Merchant Shipping Act 1970 provides that '. . . the master shall make arrangements for securing that any medical attention on board the ship is given either by him or under his supervision by a person appointed by him for the purpose'.

Regulations made under Section 24 of the same Act may require certain ships to carry specified medicines and other stores including books containing instructions and advice.

The issue of confidentiality might give rise to difficulty. The GMC do not make specific reference to ships' doctors but the general principles which they lay down in respect of occupational medicine should apply. Para 86 of the April 1987 edition of the GMC blue booklet makes reference to 'Special problems in relation to confidentiality' which 'can arise in circumstances where doctors have responsibilities to both patients and third parties . . .' The BMA *Handbook of Medical Ethics* makes specific reference to ships' surgeons (paras 2.36-2.37) and to doctors in the armed forces (paras 2.32-2.35). The point is made that the duty of confidentiality can be modified in these circumstances.

5.2   Prison Doctors

The Prison Medical Service pre-dated the National Health Service and its independence was consolidated by the enactment of the Prison Act 1952, Section 7 of which provides that each prison must have a medical officer who must be a registered medical practitioner as defined under the Medical Act 1983.

Both in England and Wales, where the Prison Department is administered by the Home Office, and in Scotland, where it is the responsibility of the Scottish Home and Health Department, there are full-time and part-time prison medical officers. Full-time prison doctors are civil servants on the Civil Service Medical Officer grade. Part-time prison medical officers are usually general practitioners in the locality who are contracted for service on the basis of an average hourly commitment per week. Where there is no full-time doctor, the part-time medical officer is 'in full medical charge'. The prison medical service also engages the services of other general practitioners and consultants (usually psychiatrists, but also physicians and surgeons) on a casual basis.

5.2.1   Duties of Medical Officers

The Prison Rules (S.I. 1964 No.388), Rule 17(1) states 'the medical officer of a prison shall have the care of the health, mental and physical, of the prisoners in that prison'. The BMA states that apart from not being able to choose their own doctor, prisoners have a right to the same medical attention as any other member of society, and a prison medical officer's responsibility to, and professional relationship with, his patients are the same as any doctor working outside prison.

The Prison Rules set out specific duties which the medical officer must perform in the case of any prisoner whose health is likely to be injuriously affected by any condition of imprisonment. The medical officer is required to pay special attention to any prisoner whose mental condition appears to require it, and make any special arrangements which appear necessary for his supervision or care.

The medical officer must also by virtue of Rule 18(3) '. . . inform the governor if he suspects any prisoner of having suicidal intentions'. The medical form completed on admission invites the medical officer to comment on possible suicidal intent.

In the case of R v Secretary of State for Home Affairs and others ex p Dew ex 16/2/87 (Law Society Gazette 1987) a prisoner applied for a judicial review. At the time of his arrest he had sustained a bullet wound and he claimed he had not received adequate medical care as required by Rules 17 and 18. Before the case was heard all the treatment requested had been provided and for procedural reasons the case did not continue.

Rule 21(5) imposes on the medical officer special duties in relation to prisoners' food and food in this context includes drink. 'The medical officer shall regularly inspect the food both before and after it is cooked, and shall report any deficiency or defect to the governor.' Food must be '. . . wholesome, nutritious, well prepared and served, reasonably varied and sufficient in quality'.

5.2.2 Other Responsibilities

Medical officers in prisons also have responsibilities concerning the issue of when prisoners should have to take exercise, work, be shaved or have their hair cut and be permitted to have alcohol. Special provision is made in relation to prisoners who are pregnant. The provision of needles to known drug addicts is currently under discussion and the medical officer may be called upon to exercise clinical judgement.

5.2.3 Accessibility/Choice

The Prison Rules (S.I. 1964 No.388), as amended, deal with such issues as accessibility of prisoners to medical treatment, and the duties of prison doctors. The Detention Centre Rules (S.I. 1983 No.569) and the Youth Custody Centre Rules (S.I. 1983 No.570) make similar provision for those institutions.

Prison Rule 17(2) provides that 'every request by a prisoner to see the medical officer shall be recorded by the officer to whom it is made and promptly passed on to the medical officer'.

Rule 17(3) states that 'the medical officer may call another medical practitioner into consultation at his discretion, and shall do so if time permits before performing any serious operation'.

The prisoner cannot, except to the limited extent set out below, choose to be treated by his own or any outside doctor.

Rule 17(4) provides that if an unconvicted prisoner wants to see an outside doctor or dentist and is prepared to pay any resulting expense the governor may (not must) allow the prisoner to be visited and treated by the outside practitioner in consultation with the medical officer. A prisoner could of course write to his doctor under the general provisions regarding prisoners' letters under Rule 34. Prison Rule 37A also provides that a prisoner who is a party to legal proceedings may see a registered medical practitioner for the purpose of being examined in connection with those proceedings. Reasonable facilities must be provided for the examination which must take place within the sight but not the hearing of a prison officer.

5.2.4   Consent to Treatment

There is no rule of law which alters the position of prisoners in this respect. However, because of the situation a prisoner is in it has been alleged that prisoners can be pressurised to agree to treatments or not to resist having them for fear of reprisal or hope of advantage in the form of parole etc. The case of Freeman v Home Office [1984] 1 AER 1036 CA arose when a prisoner sued for damages for trespass to the person on the grounds that a medical officer employed by the prison authorities, together with other prison officers, had administered drugs to him by force against his consent. The prisoner argued that the drugs were not for the relief of mental illness but for control and therefore he could not validly consent to taking them as the medical officer was in effect acting not as such but as a disciplinarian. He also argued that consent to be valid had to be informed. The appeal court, holding first that the doctrine of informed consent formed no part of English law, then went on to say that the trial judge had been right to find on the facts that the prisoner had consented to the administration of the drugs. The prisoner's claim did not succeed.

In case there is any doubt on the issue there is no legal right to administer drugs to a prisoner without his consent and for the purposes of sedation as an aid to discipline. Also the BMA *Handbook of Medical Ethics* states (para 6.21) that it is unethical for a doctor to administer a drug to a prisoner for any purpose other than for his clinical care.

The BMA *Handbook of Medical Ethics*, also states (para 4.9) that it is unethical to carry out a research procedure on a prisoner if it is of no direct benefit to the prisoner. This is because the prisoner might expect to derive some benefit from agreeing to participate, thus raising the inference that the consent had been obtained by undue influence.

5.2.5   Force Feeding

The question of whether prisoners who do not want to eat should be force fed has given rise to difficulties. At one time it was considered that the common law duty of prison doctors to preserve the health and lives of prisoners (Leigh v Gladstone [1909] 26 TLR 139) obliged them to force feed. The existence of such a duty or power is now doubted and the Secretary of State has issued guidance to prison doctors on this issue. The guidance is that:

'the common law duty of persons in charge of a prisoner is to take such steps as are reasonable in the circumstances of each case to preserve the life and health of the prisoner. This means that whilst adequate food and drink must be available to a prisoner, there is generally no duty to force him to take it against his will.'

The attention of the Governor and the medical officer will often be drawn to a prisoner who is refusing food by their examination of the record of returned food (Standing Order 2B 2). In other cases the staff of the establishment will report to the Governor and medical officer their observation that a prisoner appears not to be taking food or fluids or that he has announced an intention not to do so.

The prisoner will normally be admitted to a single room in the prison hospital either

'(a) if the prisoner's reported refusal of food continues for more than a few days and

    i if examination shows that there has been a significant loss in weight; or

    ii if ketonuria (the presence in the urine of ketones which indicates that the body has begun to metabolise its own tissue) is found; or

    iii if the prisoner appears mentally disturbed or ill; or

(b) if it is reported that he is refusing fluids,'

and a standard form should be completed and submitted to Headquarters (Medical Directorate).'

The guidance also indicates that primary responsibility for the handling of prisoners refusing food and drink rests with the medical officer. There is no rule of practice requiring any MO to resort to artificial feeding, but the guidance says that if the prisoner continues with his food refusal and his weight falls a worrying amount, or his health appears in danger of being impaired, an outside consultant should be invited to examine the prisoner. If the consultant confirms that the prisoner's capacity for rational judgement is unimpaired by illness, mental or physical, the medical officer should tell the prisoner that he will continue to receive medical supervision and advice; and that food and fluids will be made available to him; but that there is no rule of practice which requires any medical officer to resort to artificial feeding; and that the consequent and inevitable deterioration in his health may be allowed to continue without medical intervention unless he specifically requests it.

If the prisoner's capacity for rational judgement is found to be impaired by illness, mental or physical, the medical officer should take such action as he considers necessary.

This is in line with the BMA *Handbook of Medical Ethics* which quotes the Declaration of Tokyo as stating that where the prisoner's refusal is rational, which should be confirmed by at least one independent doctor, the prisoner should not be force fed although the consequences of refusal of food should be explained.

5

Section 28 of the Prison Act 1952 states that the Secretary of State may temporarily discharge a prisoner on account of self-inflicted ill health but specifically adds that the existence of such power does not detract from the medical officer's duties *vis-à-vis* any such prisoner whom the Secretary of State decides not to discharge on this ground. It should also be noted that Section 22(2)(b) of the Prison Act 1952 as amended also provides that the Secretary of State may, if satisfied that a prisoner requires medical investigation or observation or medical or surgical treatment, direct the prisoner to be taken to a hospital or other suitable place for the purposes of that treatment. The prisoner is to be kept in custody unless the Secretary of State directs to the contrary.

5.2.6   Punishments

The position of prison doctors *vis-à-vis* prison punishments etc must be considered. The Prison Rules oblige such doctors to be involved in the processes of removing prisoners from association, placing prisoners under restraint and cellular confinement. To what extent might such involvement conflict with a doctor's ethical duty?

Rule 43 deals with the right of the governor to remove a particular prisoner from association with the others. This power exists, not as a punishment, but to protect the prisoner being removed or to maintain order. The rule provides, however, that the governor shall arrange for such a prisoner to resume association 'if in any case the medical officer so advises on medical grounds'.

An award of 'cellular confinement', however, is a punishment and under Rule 53(2) shall not be made unless the medical officer has certified that the prisoner is in a fit state of health to be so dealt with. The BMA *Handbook of Medical Ethics* (para 6.20) states that a doctor would be acting unethically if he certified a prisoner as fit to undergo incarceration in a dark cell. Confinement as such is considered acceptable but the BMA view is that if a doctor is asked to examine a prisoner who is subject to close confinement the doctor must decide if the procedure is excessive and dangerous to the prisoner's health and, if so, make a written report and then refuse to be further associated with the procedure.

Under Rule 46 the governor may order a prisoner to be put under restraint 'where this is necessary to prevent the prisoner from injuring himself, or others, damaging property or creating a disturbance'.

Notice of such order must, however, be given without delay to the medical officer who must inform the governor if he concurs in that order. The governor must give effect to any recommendation which the medical officer may make. Prisoners must not otherwise be placed under restraint unless this is done for their safe custody in transit or on medical grounds and on the direction of the medical officer. This too is not meant to be a punishment. The BMA, accepting that individual restraint may be necessary for violent prisoners who are a threat to other prisoners, their guardians or themselves, states that a doctor 'may give medical advice on individual restraint where the doctor judges that the clinical condition of a prisoner makes restraint necessary' (BMA *Handbook of Medical Ethics*, para 6.21).

The BMA guidance to doctors on torture (*The Torture Report*, BMA, 1986) should also be noted and the provisions of Section 17 of the Prisons Act 1952 which states that:

'The medical officer of a prison shall not apply any painful test to a prisoner for the purpose of detecting malingering or for any other purpose except with the permission of the (Secretary of State) or the visiting committee or, as the case may be, the board of visitors.'

Even if any of the above did see fit to authorise any such tests any medical officer proposing to carry them out would be well advised to consult his defence organisation first.

5.3 Doctors in the Armed Forces

In subchapter 9.2.3 it is pointed out that only a fully registered medical practitioner may hold an appointment as physician, surgeon, or other medical officer in the naval, military or air services.

The ethical position of doctors in the Armed Services is considered in the BMA *Handbook of Medical Ethics* (paras 2.33–2.35) where the extent to which the general duty of confidentiality (see chapter 2) may be modified in such circumstances is examined.

In the book Mason JK, McCall Smith RA, *Law and Medical Ethics*, 2nd Edition, London: Butterworths, 1987 on page 131 the authors state: 'Much loose talk is often voiced as to the status of medical officers in the Armed Forces. In reality, their relationship to individual patients is precisely the same as in civilian practice, with the *proviso* that the doctor's duty to society is accentuated when this is formulated as a duty to the fighting unit; eventually the lives of many are dependent upon the health of individuals. There is, thus, a wider justification for disclosure than exists in civilian life and the serviceman has tacitly accepted this in enlisting; nevertheless the principle of justification remains valid.'

The argument seems to be that by joining the Armed Forces the patient tacitly agrees that the normal duty of confidentiality which a doctor owes to a patient can in his case be modified. However it is clear that any breach of confidentiality would have to be justifiable. The GMC in their 1987 blue booklet (paras 82-86) deal with the issue of confidentiality in a number of contexts. Armed Forces doctors are not mentioned specifically but there are comments about the special problems that can arise when a doctor has a duty to patients and to third parties (para 86).

5.4 Abortion

The general position is that it is a criminal offence for anyone other than a registered medical practitioner to perform an abortion and the latter may do so only if certain criteria are adhered to.

Section 58 of the Offences Against the Person Act 1861 states: '. . . whosoever, with intent to procure the miscarriage of any woman, whether she be or be not with child, shall unlawfully administer to her or cause to be taken by her any poison or other noxious thing, or shall unlawfully use any instrument or other means whatsoever with the like intent . . .' is guilty of an offence carrying life imprisonment.

The Infant Life (Preservation) Act 1929 (not applicable in Scotland and Northern Ireland) states in Section 1(1) '. . . any person who, with intent to destroy the life of a child capable of being born alive, by any wilful act causes a child to die before it has an existence independent of its mother, shall be guilty of felony, to wit, of child destruction'. The maximum penalty is life imprisonment. But the prosecution must prove that '. . . the act which caused the death of the child was not done in good faith for the purpose only of preserving the life of the mother'. Section 1(2) states 'evidence that a woman had at any material time been pregnant for a period of twenty-eight weeks or more shall be prima facie proof that she was at that time pregnant of a child capable of being born alive'.

It should be noted that the issue as to whether selective reduction of pregnancy, ie the reduction of fertilised ova in the course of treatment for infertility, is a criminal offence under either Act is a matter of academic debate. Doctors wishing to carry out such procedures should take advice first from their defence organisations.

The Abortion Act 1967 as amended (not applicable in Northern Ireland) affords a defence for registered medical practitioners performing an abortion provided that the following conditions are observed.

1 Two registered medical practitioners must be of the opinion, formed in good faith (Section 1(1)):

'(a) that the continuance of the pregnancy would involve risk to the life of the pregnant woman, or of injury to the physical or mental health of the pregnant woman or any existing children of her family, greater than if the pregnancy were terminated'. In determining whether any injury to health is likely account may be taken of the pregnant woman's actual or reasonably foreseeable environment. Or

'(b) that there is a substantial risk that if the child were born it would suffer from such physical or mental abnormalities as to be seriously handicapped.'

See later for provisions about how the above mentioned opinions must be certified.

2 Section 1(3) stipulates that the abortion must be carried out in a National Health Service hospital or in a place approved for the purpose by the

Minister of Health or the Secretary of State. See later for the duty to notify that the abortion has taken place.

5.4.1 Emergencies

If there is an emergency then a doctor may perform an abortion in a place which is not authorised as above and without first getting the two opinions referred to above. The criteria are set out in Section 1(4) and apply in a case where a registered medical practitioner:

'. . . is of the opinion formed in good faith, that the termination is immediately necessary to save the life or to prevent grave permanent injury to the physical or mental health of the pregnant woman.'

5.4.2 Certificates and Duty to Notify

The Abortion Regulations (S.I. 1968 No.390) (as amended) provide the following. In non-emergency cases the opinions of the two registered medical practitioners must be given in the form set out in the Schedule to the Regulations and must be obtained before the abortion is performed. In emergency cases the opinion of the doctor concerned must also be obtained in the prescribed certificate form, also before the operation, unless same is 'not reasonably practicable', in which case the certificate must be signed within 24 hours. Both types of certificate must be retained by the signing doctor for a period of three years.

The doctor who performs the abortion must within seven days of doing so give notice of same together with other information as specified in the Schedule to the Regulations to the Chief Medical Officer, DHSS. The information must be sent in a sealed envelope and must not be disclosed to any other person except the following:

(a) For the purposes of carrying out their duties an officer of the Ministry of Health authorised by the Chief Medical Officer of same or the Registrar General or authorised member of his staff.

(b) To the Director of Public Prosecutions in relation to his duty to prosecute persons who breach the abortion laws.

(c) To a police officer not below the rank of superintendent or authorised by same for the same purpose as above.

(d) For the purposes of criminal proceedings which have already begun.

(e) For *bona fide* scientific research.

(f) To the practitioner who terminated the pregnancy.

(g) To a practitioner with the consent in writing of the woman who had the abortion.

(h) To the President of the GMC so that any allegation of professional misconduct can be investigated.

It is a criminal offence to breach the provision of these regulations.

5.4.3 Conscientious Objection

Section 4 of the Abortion Act provides that no person is under a contractual or statutory duty to participate in any treatment authorised by the Act to which he has a conscientious objection. (The burden of proving that he has such an objection would lie on him if any legal proceedings were brought.) However, the above does not affect any duty to participate in treatment which is necessary to save the life or to prevent grave permanent injury to the physical or mental health of a pregnant woman.

5.4.4 Advertisements

The Medicines (Labelling and Advertising to the Public) Regulations 1978 provide that it is a criminal offence to issue an advertisement which is likely to lead to the use except under the instructions of a doctor or dentist of any medicinal product (see glossary for the definition) or any other substance or article for the purpose of procuring the miscarriage of a woman.

5.5 Doctors and Mentally Ill Patients

The Mental Health Act 1983 (not applicable in Scotland and Northern Ireland) sets out the bases on which a mentally ill person may be lawfully detained and treated in a psychiatric hospital without his consent. The Act also provides for the reception of mentally ill patients into guardianship (see later for details of what this involves). Apart from the rights of police officers to remove mentally ill persons to a place of safety (Sections 135 and 136) all compulsory admissions to psychiatric hospital and receptions into guardianship must be backed by some form of medical recommendations.

There are a number of different routes by which a patient may be lawfully detained in hospital and the procedures are different if the patient is accused of a criminal offence. The authorising sections for patients who are not before the criminal courts are briefly as follows. Section 2, admission for assessment: duration maximum 28 days. Section 4, emergency admission (this enables a patient to be admitted for assessment on the basis of only one medical recommendation but the authority will only last for 72 hours unless the second recommendation is obtained within that time). Section 3, admission for treatment: duration maximum six months.

Section 7 deals with reception into guardianship: maximum duration six months. The effect of such reception is that the patient's guardian has the right to require the patient to reside at a particular place and to attend at specified places for the purposes of medical treatment, occupation, education or training. The guardian also has power to require access to the patient to be given at his place of residence to a registered medical practitioner, approved social worker or other specified person.

Different medical criteria apply for each type of admission and reception and there is not space here to specify these. However, in the case of non-criminal admissions there must be two medical recommendations made in the prescribed form and the form states what the relevant criteria are. The definitions of 'mental disorder' and 'severe medical impairment' are not, however, reproduced on the forms although they are specifically defined in the Act as follows.

In Section 1 'mental disorder' is stated to mean 'mental illness, arrested or incomplete development of mind, psychopathic disorder and other disorder or disability of mind'. 'Severe mental impairment' is stated to mean 'a state of arrested or incomplete development of mind which includes severe impairment of intelligence and social functioning and is associated with abnormally aggressive or seriously irresponsible conduct on the part of the person concerned'.

The provisions of Section 12, which sets out certain general rules in relation to medical recommendations, should also be noted. These provide:

1   The recommendations must be signed on or before the date of the application to admit, or to receive the patient into guardianship.

2   The doctors must have personally examined the patient either together or separately but in the latter event no more than five days must elapse between the two examinations.

3   One recommendation must be given by a practitioner approved by the Secretary of State as having special experience in the treatment of mental disorder and unless that person has previous acquaintance with the patient the other doctor should 'if practicable' have such acquaintance. There are other provisions which stipulate that one, but only one, of the doctors making the recommendation can be on the staff of the hospital to which the patient is to be admitted. (For these purposes a doctor employed part-time in the hospital is not deemed to be a practitioner on its staff.) These provisions are phrased not to apply if the hospital is a mental nursing home or if the patient is to be in private patient's accommodation, in which case Section 12(5)(e) effectively provides that neither of the recommendations can be made by a doctor on the staff of the admitting hospital. However, if strict adherence to these requirements in the case of National Health Service admissions would result in delay which would in turn result in serious risk to the health and safety of the patient, then provided one doctor works at the proposed admitting hospital less than half his contracted time to the National Health Service this provision need not be adhered to unless one of the signing doctors is a consultant and the other works in a grade where he is under that consultant's direction (whatever the location).

5

Certain doctors are barred from making medical recommendations because of the relationship they bear either to the other signing doctor or to the patient. The following may not make a recommendation.

1 The person applying to admit the patient (usually a close relative).

2 A partner of that applicant.

3 A partner of the other doctor making the recommendation.

4 A person employed as an assistant by the applicant or the other signing doctor.

5 A person who receives or has an interest in the receipt of any payment made on account of the maintenance of the patient.

6 The following relatives of the patient may not make the recommendation: husband, wife, father-in-law, mother-in-law, son, son-in-law, daughter, daughter-in-law, brother, brother-in-law, sister or sister-in-law.

7 Anyone who is related as in '6' to anyone in categories 1-5 may not make the recommendation.

8 Anyone who is related as in '6' to the other doctor making the recommendation may not make the second recommendation.

All the above relates to patients being admitted to psychiatric hospital not via the criminal courts. In the latter case the procedures are different. Briefly the various sections which give the courts the power to admit mentally ill offenders (or in some cases those accused only of criminal offences) to hospital are as follows.

Section 35 enables the court to remand an accused person to psychiatric hospital to obtain a report on his mental condition. The person can be so remanded for up to 28 days at a time not exceeding 12 weeks in all. The court must receive written or oral evidence from a registered medical practitioner.

Section 36 enables a person awaiting trial (who might otherwise be remanded in custody) to be remanded to a psychiatric hospital for treatment. The time limits are the same as above as is the requirement for medical evidence. Only the Crown Court may make such an order. Section 37 enables the court to make hospital or guardianship orders in respect of mentally ill offenders. The effect is the same as if the person had been admitted for treatment or received into guardianship as above. The court must have written or oral evidence from two doctors. Section 38 states that the court may make interim hospital orders for up to 12 weeks (28 day extensions can then be obtained for a maximum overall of six months).

Section 41 gives the Crown Court power to add to a hospital order a restriction order with or without limit of time. The effect of this is that whilst the restriction order lasts the patient cannot be given leave of absence, discharged from hospital or transferred without permission of the Secretary of State. In such cases at least one of the doctors must give oral evidence. In all cases at least one of the doctors who give evidence to the court must be approved as having special experience in the diagnosis or treatment of mental disorder.

The Act also provides for the compulsory detention in a psychiatric hospital of patients who are there on a voluntary basis and for the continuation of the authority to detain patients admitted under the above provisions.

By Section 5 the registered medical practitioner in charge of the patient's treatment may furnish a report to the hospital managers who may then authorise the detention of a patient for up to 72 hours. In the case of patients detained under a section it is the duty of the responsible medical officer to examine the patient within two months of the date when the authority to detain is due to end and, if appropriate and if certain medical criteria apply which warrant continued detention, to provide a report to the managers. The doctor must consult with one or more persons who have been professionally concerned with the patient's medical treatment. There are similar provisions in relation to guardianship.

The Act provides for many categories of detained patients to apply to the Mental Health Review Tribunal for discharge from their section and also for the automatic reference of some patients whose detention has been continued. The tribunal will require a medical report in most cases and it is worth noting that a copy of same will be sent to the patient unless the tribunal is satisfied that to do so would adversely affect the health or welfare of the patient.

Normally, of course, a doctor may not treat a patient without the latter giving informed consent to the specific treatment in question. Before the passing of the Mental Health Act 1983 there was some controversy about the imposition of treatment on unwilling detained patients and about the lack of safeguards when operations such as leucotomies were being performed. The 1983 Act now makes specific provision for the obtaining of a second opinion in circumstances where certain types of operation are to be performed even if the patient has consented to same and where a patient objects to having certain sorts of treatment. The provisions in the Act which deal with the issue of consent to treatment apply to all patients detained in pursuance of the Act except the following.

1   Patients admitted under the emergency provisions who are still awaiting the second medical opinion.

2   Patients who were in hospital on a voluntary basis and who are now being detained following the submission of their doctor's report to the managers (there is a similar holding power for nurses of up to six hours and these patients are also not covered by the provisions).

3   Patients remanded under Section 35 for a report on their mental condition.

4   Patients admitted under Sections 135 and 136 pursuant to police powers.

5

5   Patients in respect of whom the criminal courts have made hospital orders but who are currently waiting in a place of safety (usually a prison) for a hospital place.

6   Conditionally discharged patients who have not been recalled to hospital.

The consent to treatment provisions also apply to all patients who are not liable to be detained and 'patient' in the context is defined in Section 145 as a person suffering or appearing to be suffering from mental disorder.

By virtue of Section 57 the following types of treatment, when applied to those categories of patient to whom the consent to treatment provision applies, must be given only if the patient consents and a second opinion (see later for details) has been obtained.

'(a) Any surgical operation for destroying brain tissue or for destroying the functioning of brain tissue; and'

(b) Any other treatment specified in statutory Regulations. The only such treatment specified at the moment (in The Mental Health (Hospital, Guardianship and Consent to Treatment) Regulations (S.I. 1983 No 893)) is the surgical implantation of hormones for the purpose of reducing male sexual drive.

The 'second opinion' must consist of the following. A registered medical practitioner who must not be the doctor in charge of the patient's treatment and who must be specially appointed by the Secretary of State for these purposes plus two other persons also specially appointed who must certify in writing that the patient is capable of understanding the nature, purpose and likely effects of the treatment in question and has consented to it.

The registered medical practitioner must also certify in writing that, having regard to the likelihood of the treatment alleviating or preventing a deterioration of the patient's condition, the treatment should be given. The practitioner must consult with two other persons professionally concerned with the patient's treatment, one of whom must be a nurse and the other must not be a nurse or a doctor.

Other types of treatment require either the consent of the patient or a second opinion (Section 58). These are:

(a) any treatment specified in Regulations. So far the Regulations referred to above have only specified electroconvulsive therapy (ECT) and

(b) the administration of medicine at any time during a period when a patient is liable to be detained if three months have elapsed since the medicine was first given.

For these categories of treatment to be lawful either the patient must consent and a registered medical practitioner specially appointed as above must state in writing that the patient is capable of understanding the nature, purpose and likely effects of the treatment and has consented to it; or

The specially appointed doctor, who must not be the doctor in charge of the patient's treatment, must certify in writing that the patient is not capable of understanding the nature, purpose and likely effects of the treatment or has not consented to it but that having regard to the likelihood of the treatment alleviating or preventing a deterioration of his condition the treatment should be given. The doctor must as above consult with other professionals.

The above provisions of Sections 57 and 58 do not apply in situations of urgency as defined in Section 62 as follows, ie to any treatment which:

(a) is immediately necessary to save the patient's life; or

(b) (not being irreversible) is immediately necessary to prevent a serious deterioration in the patient's condition; or

(c) (not being irreversible or hazardous) is immediately necessary to alleviate serious suffering by the patient; or

(d) (not being irreversible or hazardous) is immediately necessary to prevent the patient from behaving violently or being a danger to himself or others.

It should also be noted that there are various provisions concerning plans of treatment and the withdrawal of consent by the patient.

5

Lastly, Section 63 states that medical treatments for mental disorder which do not come within the ambit of Sections 57 and 58 can be given lawfully without the consent of the patient provided that they are given by or under the direction of the responsible medical officer. The fact that there is no express statutory provision whereby another person may consent to treatment for a physical condition on behalf of a mentally ill person has been discussed in subchapter 1.6, The Patient with Mental Illness or Mental Handicap.

The final provision of the Mental Health Act which might be of particular interest to doctors is that set out in Section 139. This provides that (in the case of individuals only) no civil or criminal proceedings can be brought against any person in respect of any act purporting to be done in pursuance of the Act or Regulations unless that act was done in bad faith or without reasonable care. Additionally no civil proceedings may be brought unless leave of the High Court is first obtained and no prosecution may be commenced in the criminal courts without the consent of the Director of Public Prosecutions.

6 Medical Negligence

If one person has behaved negligently towards another then it may be possible for that other to sue for damages in the civil courts. However, to mount such an action successfully the person aggrieved will have to establish (on the balance of probabilities) a number of elements. Firstly a legal duty of care must be owed by the alleged wrong-doer to the victim. Secondly the former must have behaved negligently, ie his behaviour must have fallen short of the standard required by law and it must have been reasonably foreseeable that the careless behaviour in question could damage the plaintiff. A causal link between the behaviour and the damage in question must also be proved and some damage must have been suffered.

There is no doubt that a doctor owes a duty of care to a patient he is treating whether privately or under the National Health Service.

Halsbury's Laws Volume 30, para 34 states 'a person who holds himself out as ready to give medical advice or treatment impliedly undertakes that he is possessed of skill and knowledge for the purpose'; and in para 35 'the practitioner must bring to the task a reasonable degree of skill and knowledge and must exercise a reasonable degree of care'.

The question as to at what point a doctor can be said to have behaved negligently has given rise to some difficulty. Not every medical mishap gives the patient the right to sue for damages. This is an ever changing field of law.

In a series of cases it has been established that if a doctor treats a patient in a way that is considered acceptable at the time by one responsible body of medical opinion the doctor cannot be held to be negligent even if there is another responsible body of medical opinion which considers the treatment in question was wrong.

In the case of Bolam v Friern Barnet HMC [1957] 2 AER 118, for instance, a patient to whom ECT was administered sustained fractures. No relaxant drugs or manual restraints were used. At the time there were two bodies of opinion within the profession, one in favour of the use of relaxant drugs and one against and there were also two opinions as to whether in the absence of relaxants, manual control should be applied. The doctor was therefore absolved from negligence. In the headnote to the case it is stated:

The jury were directed '(i) a doctor is not negligent, if he is acting in accordance with a practice accepted as proper by a responsible body of medical men skilled in that particular art, merely because there is a body of such opinion that takes a contrary view'.

In the case of Whitehouse v Jordan [1981] 1 AER 267 damages were claimed after a baby was born with brain damage after a senior hospital registrar had pulled the fetus several times with obstetric forceps, the baby being delivered eventually by Caesarean section. The House of Lords upheld the Court of Appeal's rejection of the trial judge's finding of negligence, but not the Court of Appeal's conclusion that an error of clinical judgement could not in law amount to negligence. The headnote to the law report states (per Lord Edmund-Davies, Lord Fraser and Lord Russell): 'While some errors of clinical judgement may be completely consistent with the due exercise of professional skill, other acts or omissions in the course of exercising clinical judgement may be so glaringly below proper standards as to make a finding of negligence inevitable. The test whether a surgeon has been negligent is whether he has failed to measure up in any respect, whether in clinical judgement or otherwise to the standard of the ordinary skilled surgeon exercising and professing to have the special skill of a surgeon'. The last sentence probably states the position so far as is possible.

The principles of 'vicarious liability' (discussed in subchapter 9.6 in relation to indemnity schemes) should also be noted in relation to negligence. If a doctor is employed by someone else that employer can also be sued if the doctor is negligent. Conversely a general practitioner who employs staff can be held legally responsible for his employees' negligent actions.

In the following paragraphs we consider the legal position (*vis-à-vis* negligence claims) of junior hospital doctors and medical students doing clinical work. Also discussed is the duty of doctors who suddenly come across the scene of an accident and the duties of general practitioners to refer their patients to specialists (with special reference to the problems caused by National Health Service waiting lists).

6.1 Junior Hospital Doctors

Junior hospital doctors owe a duty to their patients not to be negligent and can be sued if their care of a patient falls below a legally acceptable standard. The issue of just what standard ought to be expected was considered by the Court of Appeal in the case of Wilsher v Essex AHA [1987] 2 WLR 425. A baby born three months prematurely was being treated in a specialist unit. In order to monitor the level of oxygen in the blood a house officer inserted a catheter but put it into a vein instead of an artery. His senior registrar failed to realise what had happened and later inserted another catheter also mistakenly into a vein. As a result, it was alleged, the baby received too much oxygen and his sight was seriously impaired. (The facts were somewhat more complex than this but there is not space to go into them more fully.) A number of legal issues were raised.

One point which was argued by the AHA (note the application of the principle of vicarious liability – they were being sued because of the actions of their employees) was that special consideration should be given to the need for the Health Service to allow young doctors and nurses to learn on the job and that these inexperienced staff should not be expected to demonstrate the same standard of patient care as their more experienced counterparts. The court by a majority rejected this argument. We quote from the headnote to the case report:

'The court did not apply a standard of care reasonably to be expected of a specialist care unit but it considered the acts of the individual doctors attached to the unit and whether they had performed to the standard reasonably to be expected of professional men holding the post they occupied in that unit but without regard to the fact that inexperienced doctors gaining knowledge of a specialist branch of medicine were necessarily employed in the National Health Service'. And 'that the senior registrar should have appreciated that the X-rays showed that the catheter was not situated in an artery and in failing to do so he had been negligent; that the junior doctor had been entitled to rely on his work being checked by the senior registrar and in all the circumstances no finding of negligence should be made against him'.

The defendants having failed in the Court of Appeal appealed to the House of Lords. The appeal was allowed in 1988 but on the basis of a different legal point. The opinion of the majority of the Court of Appeal, although legally no longer binding, remains persuasive and likely to be followed in future cases which would probably say that if a person is selected to fill a post in a hospital then regardless of his actual experience he must do the work to the standard that should reasonably be expected of a person in such a position. However, a junior doctor, it seems, is entitled to rely on his work being checked by his seniors.

Conversely, a junior doctor who chose to depart from the instruction he was given by his senior could find himself vulnerable to a negligence action if anything went wrong.

6.2 Medical Students Doing Clinical Work

The following guidance concerning the employment of medical students in hospital has been given by the Government (but note that the Medical Act referred to has now been replaced by Section 47 of the Medical Act 1983).

The Medical Acts 1956 and 1978

A DHSS letter to Regional Health Authorities in September 1971 (DS 256/71) stated the following.

'4   By virtue of Section 28(1) of the Medical Act 1956 as amended by Schedule 7 to the Medical Act 1978, an appointment as physician, surgeon or medical officer in a National Health Service hospital can only be held by a person registered with the GMC. Undergraduates are unable, therefore, to hold such appointments. Medical Students however, are able to undertake voluntary work or when covering for an absent house officer because of holidays or sickness.

Conditions under which students do clinical work

5   In view of the advice contained in paragraph 4 above, Health Authorities should ensure that when students undertake clinical work, whether as part of their clinical course or when voluntarily assisting in hospital departments, they do so under the close supervision of a registered medical practitioner. The following conditions must be observed:-

    i   The consultant in charge, who has an overall clinical responsibility for his patients, will be responsible for ensuring supervision by a suitable named practitioner. The named practitioner must have his responsibilities clearly explained to him by the consultant in charge. It will be for this named practitioner to determine the actual degree of supervision necessary for the various clinical procedures which may be undertaken by the student. Where a student assists with a maternity case the supervision of a certified midwife is acceptable.

    ii A student should not initiate treatment for a patient on his own diagnosis; both the diagnosis and treatment must be confirmed by a registered practitioner.

    iii A student must not act as or be regarded as a 'locum' for an absent house officer. The responsibility for an absent house officer's job, if a locum tenens is not engaged, must at any one time devolve upon a named member of the medical staff, who may be assisted in covering the house officer's job as well as his own by a medical student. The practitioner who is standing in must at all times supervise the clinical activities of his student assistant.

    iv A student must not, in any circumstances, prescribe.

    v   A student should not request X-rays.

    vi Health Boards must secure the consent of the Dean of the medical school or his authorised representative before allowing a medical student to act as an assistant. Health Boards will wish to discuss with Deans the most convenient arrangements for this (where it is not already done).'

It is feared that at present the guidance set out in the DHSS letter (DS 256/71) is not being heeded and unqualified locums are being placed in positions in which suitable supervision is not available. There do not appear to be any decided cases at present concerning negligence of a student but any student taking on such a post should heed the observations in the Wilsher case (see subchapter 6.1). On page 441 in that case one judge in the Court of Appeal observed 'to my mind this notion of a duty tailored to the actor, rather than to the act which he elects to perform has no place in the law of tort'. It is highly likely that a student who 'elected' to take on a post which should be filled by a qualified doctor would be expected to perform with the expertise of such a doctor. It is likely also that the health authority would be considered negligent for placing a student in such a post. (This too was noted in the Wilsher case.)

Consultants and others should note that improper delegation to a medical student could give rise to a finding of negligence against the delegator.

6.3 Coming Upon the Scene of an Accident

A doctor who suddenly comes across the scene of an accident might be in some dilemma as to the extent of his responsibilities in such a situation. In England both the criminal and the civil law have been concerned overwhelmingly with protecting the individual from wrongful acts as opposed to wrongful omissions. To quote one academic: 'There is no general duty to act positively for the benefit of others. An adult who stands by and watches a child (to whom he stands in no special relationship) drown in a foot of water may have to answer before some higher tribunal somewhere, sometime, but he is not accountable for negligence in the English court, though he has omitted to do what most men would for others'. (See Rogers WVH ed. *Winfield and Jolowicz on Tort*, 12th ed. London: Sweet and Maxwell, 1984, page 80.)

A person who comes across the scene of an accident and decides to do nothing to assist the victim could not therefore in general be prosecuted for the crimes of manslaughter or assault nor could he be sued in the civil courts for negligence.

The person could be held responsible, however, if he had some sort of special relationship with the victim, eg if he was the parent or guardian of the drowning child referred to above.

There is no statute or as yet decided common law case to the effect that a doctor as such coming across an unconscious individual with whom the doctor has no connection whatever is by virtue of his position as a doctor under a duty to assist that person. This is a peculiarity of the common law in the UK. In virtually every other legal system, especially within the EEC, it is a serious offence under the penal code not to offer assistance and is heavily penalised.

However, a general practitioner coming across an unconscious person within his own practice area might be in breach of his National Health Service terms of service if he did not assist. The National Health Service (General Medical and Pharmaceutical Services) Regulations (S.I. 1974 No.160) (as amended) Schedule 1 Part 1 states in paragraph 4 that a doctor's patients include 'persons to whom he may be requested to give treatment which is immediately required owing to an accident or other emergency at any place in his practice area'.

6

There are exceptions to this requirement, for example for elderly infirm doctors.

In Scotland the National Health Service (General Medical and Pharmaceutical Services) (Scotland) Regulations (S.I. 1974 No.506) provide as follows.

Paragraph 4 (1(e)) states that the persons for whose treatment a doctor is responsible include 'all persons for whom he may be required in terms of sub-paragraph (3) to provide treatment which is immediately required in case of accident or other emergency'.

Paragraph 4 (3) further states 'if a doctor is requested to provide treatment, and is available, he shall provide treatment immediately required, by reason of accident or other emergency, by a person who is not on the list of and who has not been accepted as a temporary resident by or assigned to, any doctor practising in the locality, or who is on the list of or has been accepted as a temporary resident by or assigned to, such a doctor, but neither the said doctor nor any deputy whom he may have appointed is available'.

To deliberately walk away from a seriously ill person would no doubt be unethical. For example, the English text of the International Code of Medical Ethics states amongst other things: 'A physician shall always bear in mind the obligation of preserving human life'. (See pages 70-1 of the BMA *Handbook of Medical Ethics*.)

Once a decision is taken to intervene then the rescuer is under the usual duty to take reasonable care. 'There is authority for saying that, although a person is not normally under a duty to rescue another yet once he embarks upon the actual task of rescue, he may be liable if the method of rescue, or its abandonment leaves the other worse off than he would otherwise have been.' (See Clerk JF and Lindsell WHB, *Clerk and Lindsell on Torts*, 15th ed. London: Sweet and Maxwell, 1982, page 35.)

However, if the rescuer is injured whilst assisting then he in turn may be able to claim damages from the person responsible for the hazardous situation. (That person may of course be the victim himself.) For example, in one case a doctor died when going down a well full of fumes to rescue two workmen. His estate claimed successfully for damages for his death from the defendants whose defective system of work had lead to the accumulation of lethal gas inside the well. (See Baker and Anor v T E Hopkins and Son Ltd [1959] 1 WLR, page 966.)

For the issue of lack of consent see Chapter 1.

6.4 Referral of Patients to Specialists

The legal position regarding the referral of patients to specialists needs to be considered firstly from the point of view of the general practitioner and secondly from the point of view of the consultant and the employing authority.

6.4.1 General Practitioners

Firstly, are general practitioners bound to refer patients to specialists in the first place?

So far as National Health Service (NHS) patients are concerned there is a clear duty to do so as and when necessary. In England and Wales the National Health Service (General Medical and Pharmaceutical Services) Regulations (S.I. 1974 No.160) as amended provide for general practitioners' terms of service to include a condition that the general practitioners must give to their patients 'all necessary and appropriate personal medical services of the type usually provided by general medical practitioners'.

Later it is stated: 'Such services include arrangements for referring patients as necessary to any other services provided under the Health Services Acts'.

The BMA's ethical advice is that general practitioners should always acquiesce in any reasonable request by a patient for a second opinion.

In Scotland the National Health Service (General Medical and Pharmaceutical Services) (Scotland) Regulations (S.I. 1974 No.506) as amended also stipulate that general practitioners must give their patients all proper and necessary treatment and that: 'The doctor shall also give his patients such advice or assistance as he may consider appropriate to enable them to take advantage of other medical services available under the National Health Service'.

Whether the patient is private or National Health Service, failure to refer the patient to a specialist in circumstances where such a referral ought to have been made could result in a successful claim for negligence if the patient suffered injury as a result.

The GMC blue booklet states (para 89) what duties general practitioners are considered to have in the area of referral of patients to specialists.

Secondly, are general practitioners allowed to receive fees as a result of the referral?

In the case of NHS patients a general practitioner who charged a fee for referring these patients to a private consultant would be considered to be in breach of his terms of service (para 32).

In all cases any agreement whereby the general practitioner was to receive part of the consultant's fee (as a 'commission' for example) could result in disciplinary proceedings. Para 55 of the GMC blue booklet states that the GMC have regarded fee-splitting arrangements 'with concern'. (See also para 8.27 of the BMA *Handbook of Medical Ethics*.)

Once a general practitioner has decided to refer the patient to a specialist then the question of what responsibilities the general practitioner continues to have must be considered. The general position is that the general practitioner's duty of care towards the patient still continues. If, however, the hospital fails to give

6

the patient an appointment to see a specialist or delays for a long time in doing so then the general practitioner could be placed in a difficult position through no fault of his own. There are no fixed rules in either the common law or statute as to whether the general practitioner is under a legal duty to chase the hospital up and ensure that the patient is seen by a specialist within a reasonable time. That being so a general practitioner could only be held responsible for a delay in the patient obtaining hospital treatment if the general practitioner had been negligent applying the usual legal criteria in this respect. The sorts of situations that could lead to trouble are, for instance, failing to make sure that the hospital was made aware that the patient's condition was serious or had become so whilst the patient had been waiting to be seen by a consultant.

It should be noted in this context that in 1976 the Health Service Commissioner found that maladministration had occurred when there had been a failure to secure emergency treatment from the NHS. The Ombudsman stated that if the general practitioner had approached the consultant rather than a junior he would probably have obtained a bed for his patient.

The case of Coles v Reading HMC (*The Times*, January 31, 1963) illustrates also that the general practitioner is expected to find out exactly what treatment his patient has been given in circumstances where the patient has referred himself to hospital. In that case a man who had suffered a crushed thumb went to a cottage hospital. There he was told to go to a nearby general hospital for an anti-tetanus injection. He did not do so. He was seen later by his general practitioner, who wrongly made the assumption that as the man had been seen at a hospital he must have been given an anti-tetanus injection. The man later died and the court held that both the hospital authority and the general practitioner had been negligent, the former because they had not adequately impressed on the man the importance of having the injection and the general practitioner because he had failed to enquire as to whether adequate prophylactic treatment had in fact been given.

6.4.2 The Hospital and the Consultant

In England and Wales the National Health Service Act 1977 provides that the Secretary of State for Social Services is under a duty to: '... continue the promotion in England and Wales of a comprehensive health service designed to secure improvement

(a) in the physical and mental health of the people of those countries; and

(b) in the prevention, diagnosis and treatment of illness, and for that purpose to provide or secure the effective provision of services in accordance with this Act.'

The Act goes on to impose on the Secretary of State a duty to provide to such extent as he considers necessary to meet all reasonable requirements hospital accommodation and a wide range of other services. The problems general practitioners may encounter when a patient referred for specialist advice is kept waiting a long time have already been mentioned. In the case of R v Secretary of State for Social Services ex p Hincks 1979 (unreported) QB 24.1.79 (Court of Appeal 18.3.80) orthopaedic patients who had been kept waiting longer than was medically advisable attempted to obtain legal redress against the Government for the failure to treat them within a reasonable time. The action failed, the judge ruling that regard had to be paid to the financial limits imposed upon the Secretary of State by Parliament. Recent cases involving hole-in-the-heart babies have gone the same way.

It appears therefore that although the duty to provide hospital facilities lies with the Secretary of State, as the law stands at present, if there is not sufficient money to provide treatments under the NHS as promptly as doctors consider desirable then there is no legal basis to challenge this. (In Scotland the National Health Service (Scotland) Act 1978 makes similar provisions in respect of medical facilities.)

The converse situation is that where a consultant accepts a patient for treatment without being asked to do so by the general practitioner. It is clear from the 1987 GMC blue booklet that in general for a specialist to accept a patient without a referral from a general practitioner is considered to be a breach of medical ethics. Paragraphs 90 and 91 of the booklet make clear the duties of the specialist in these circumstances.

The BMA *Handbook of Medical Ethics* (para 2.11) lists situations in which specialists would not be acting improperly in accepting patients without such a referral.

6

In cases where a patient is accepted without a referral the GMC blue booklet sets out (paras 90–91) what action should be taken to keep the patient's general practitioner informed of what has occurred.

7 Other Activities

7.1 The Doctor as Company Director

7.1.1 Implications in Relation to Ethical Duties Not to Advertise

The GMC blue booklet (April 1987) makes it clear that for doctors to indulge in 'self-promotion' is unethical. (See paras 58-62 where the nature of the professional offence involved is set out.) Later on in this publication the GMC consider the 'circumstances in which questions of self-promotion most commonly arise'. (See paras 92-108.) One such circumstance envisaged is 'Public references to doctors by other companies or organisations'.

Para 101 states: 'The name of a doctor who is a director of a company may be shown on the company's notepaper, where that is a statutory requirement. But problems can arise if reports, notices or notepaper issued by a company or organisation with which a doctor is associated, or by which he is employed, draw attention to his attainments in a way likely to promote his professional advantage. Doctors should accordingly take steps to avoid the publication of such references, whether or not the business of their company is connected with medical practice'.

When is it a statutory requirement to name the directors? The effect of Section 305(1) of the Companies Act 1985 is that a company does not have to name any of its directors on its notepaper. However if it names one director it must name all the directors and must include in legible characters the Christian name or initials and surname of each individual and the corporate name of every corporate director. If this requirement is violated the company can be fined.

Another mandatory requirement imposed on companies in relation to publicising the identities of directors is that contained in Section 288 which obliges companies to keep at their registered office a register of directors and secretaries. The register must contain the following details about each director who is an individual:

Present Christian name and surname (and any former such name).
Usual residential address.
Nationality.
Business occupation (if any).
Particulars of other directorships.
In some cases date of birth.

This register must be open to inspection by members of the public during business hours (for at least two hours per day).

7.2 Doctors and Patent Law

The rationale behind the patents system has been described thus: 'It is desirable in the public interest that industrial techniques should be improved. In order to encourage improvement and to encourage the disclosure of improvements in preference to their use in secret, any person devising an improvement in a manufactured article, or in machinery or methods for making it, may upon disclosure of his improvement at the Patent Office demand to be given a monopoly in the use of it for a period of . . . years.' (See Banks MAL (Chairman) *British patent system; Report of the Committee to Examine the Patent System.* Cmnd 4407, London, HMSO, 1970.)

The Patents Act 1977, most of which came into force on 1 June 1978, governs applications for patents made after that date and provides that an invention can be patented for 20 years. The Patents Act 1949 governed previous patent applications and subject to some conditions those known as 'old' patents (many of which of course still exist) have had their life extended to 20 years also. Even prior to the passing of the Patents Act 1977 methods for the medical treatment of human beings were held not to be patentable as they did not fall within the concept of manufacture. Treatments which were not of a curative nature were sometimes successfully patented, for example methods of contraception, hair softening etc. The Patents Act 1977, however, makes the position quite clear. Section 1 of that Act states that an invention can only be patented if, *inter alia*, it is new, it involves an inventive step and it is capable of industrial application. Section 4 then goes on to expressly exclude medical treatment from being interpreted as being capable of industrial application.

Section 4(2) states: 'An invention of a method of treatment of the human or animal body by surgery or therapy or of diagnosis practised on the human or animal body shall not be taken to be capable of industrial application'.

Drugs and appliances were patentable previously and still are. Section 4(3) of the Patents Act 1977 makes it clear that the exclusion of medical treatment from the patent system does not extend to medicines. Section 4(3) states: 'Subsection (2) above shall not prevent a product consisting of a substance or composition being treated as capable of industrial application merely because it is invented for use in any such method' (ie method of treatment of human or animal body).

There is also an interesting proviso regarding when a substance used for medical treatment can be considered to be 'new' for the purposes of satisfying the list of criteria necessary for something to be patentable. Section 2(6) provides: 'In the case of an invention consisting of a substance or composition for use in a method of treatment of the human or animal body by surgery or therapy or of diagnosis practised on the human or animal body, the fact that the substance or composition forms part of the state of the art shall not prevent the invention from being taken to be new if the use of the substance or composition in any such method does not form part of the state of the art'.

Inventions cannot be patented if they already form part of what is termed the 'state of the art'. The Patents Act defines this phrase as being taken to '. . . comprise all matter (whether a product, a process, information about either, or anything else) which has at any time before the priority date of that invention been made available to the public (whether in the United Kingdom or elsewhere) by written or oral description, by use or in any other way'. (Section 2(2).)

When something is invented there could be a dispute over to whom the invention belongs, if the inventor was at the time in the employment of somebody else. Section 39 of the Patents Act 1977 sets out the circumstances in which an employee's inventions are to be considered in law to belong to his employer.

Section 40 provides that if the patent is considered to belong to the employer the employee can in certain circumstances apply for compensation. The application must be made during the period beginning with the date when the relevant patent is granted and ending one year after it has ceased to have effect.

7.3 Animal Experiments

Doctors are not in the main placed in any special position so far as the law relating to animal experimentation is concerned. Statute controls the performance of painful experiments on living animals, the administration of beneficial substances to animals in the course of medicinal tests, inhumane operations on animals and the practice of veterinary surgery by unqualified persons.

The Animals (Scientific Procedures) Act 1986 came into force on 1 January 1987 except for Sections 7, 10(3) and Section 29, which means the Act is not yet in force in Northern Ireland. Section 3 of the Act prohibits the carrying on of 'regulated procedures' (see below) in relation to any animal unless certain conditions are fulfilled.

Section 2 defines what is meant by a 'regulated procedure' for this purpose as follows:

'. . . any experimental or other scientific procedure applied to a protected animal which may have the effect of causing that animal pain, suffering, distress or lasting harm'. (Section 2 (1).) When considering whether any procedure might have the above mentioned effects Section 2(4) provides that '. . . the use of an anaesthetic or analgesic, decerebration and any other procedure for rendering an animal insentient shall be disregarded'. The subsection then states that the administration of same to animals for the purposes of experimental or other scientific procedures shall itself be regarded as coming within the category of regulated procedures.

Also regarded as being regulated procedures are scientific or experimental procedures applied to a protected animal if the procedure is part of a series applied to the same animal and if the series may have any of the above mentioned unpleasant effects (Section 2(2)). Included is also a procedure that might result in the birth or hatching of a protected animal if the procedure may have the above mentioned unpleasant effects (Section 2(3)).

Some procedures are excluded from the definition if certain criteria are met. Section 2(5) provides that the ringing, tagging or marking of an animal or the application of any other humane procedure for the sole purpose of enabling an animal to be identified is not a regulated procedure if it causes only momentary pain or distress and no lasting harm. Section 2(6) excludes from the definition medicinal tests on animals as defined in Section 32(6) of the Medicines Act (see subchapter 7.3.1 where the text of this definition is set out) provided the substance or article is administered in accordance with the provisions of that Act as set out in Section 32(4) or in accordance with an order under Section 35(8)(b).

Killing a protected animal is a regulated procedure only if the animal is killed for experimental or other scientific use, the place where it is killed is a designated establishment (see later) and the method employed is not one sanctioned as appropriate to that particular animal by Schedule 1 of the Act which lists standard methods for humane killing. (Section 2(7).)

It is obvious from the above that in order to know whether an experiment etc comes within the definition as being a 'regulated procedure' and is thus controlled by the Act it is necessary to know what animals come within the definition of being 'protected animals'. This point is dealt with in Section 1 which states that a protected animal means '. . . any living vertebrate other than man'.

'. . . an animal is living until the permanent cessation of circulation or the destruction of its brain' (Subsection 4).

A vertebrate means '. . . any animal of the Sub-phylum Vertebrata of the Phylum Chordata' (Subsection 5).

Subsection 2 states that a '. . . vertebrate in its foetal, larval or embryonic form is a protected animal only from the stage of its development when

(a) in the case of a mammal, bird or reptile, half the gestation or incubation period for the relevant species has elapsed; and

(b) in any other case, it becomes capable of independent feeding.'

The Secretary of State may by order extend and alter some of these provisions.

As mentioned above, Section 3 of the Act provides that a 'regulated procedure' must not be applied to any animal unless certain criteria are complied with. Contravention of Section 3 is a criminal offence although in England and Wales no prosecution can take place without the consent of the Director of Public

Prosecutions and in Scotland prosecution is at the instance of the Lord Advocate through the procurator fiscal. The criteria are as follows:

The person performing the regulated procedure must hold an appropriate personal licence, granted by the Secretary of State (Section 4). This qualifies '. . . the holder to apply specified regulated procedures to animals of specified description at a specified place'. The application must (unless the Secretary of State grants exemption from this provision) be endorsed by a person who already holds such a licence or one treated as such by transitional provisions which enable licences granted under the Cruelty to Animals Act 1876 to continue until their expiry and who '. . . has knowledge of the biological or other relevant qualifications and of the training, experience and character of the applicant'. The endorser must '. . . if practicable, be a person occupying a position of authority at a place where the applicant is to be specified by the licence to carry out the procedures authorised in it'. A licence cannot be given to someone under the age of 18 and has to be reviewed at least every five years.

Section 10(2) of the Act sets out the required conditions attached to a personal licence.

There must be in existence in relation to the regulated procedure a project licence. Section 5 states that these may be granted by the Secretary of State to specify a programme of work and authorise the application as part of that programme of specified regulated procedures to be applied to animals of a specified description at specified places. A project licence is not to be granted '. . . except to a person who undertakes overall responsibility for the programme to be specified in the licence'. Before granting such a licence the Secretary of State must be satisfied that the programme is being '...undertaken for one or more of the following purposes:

(a) the prevention (whether by the testing of any product or otherwise) or the diagnosis or treatment of disease, ill-health or abnormality, or their effects, in man, animals or plants;

(b) the assessment, detection, regulation or modification of physiological conditions in man, animals or plants;

(c) the protection of the natural environment in the interests of the health or welfare of man or animals;

(d) the advancement of knowledge in biological or behavioural sciences;

(e) education or training otherwise than in primary or secondary schools;

(f) forensic enquiries;

(g) the breeding of animals for experimental or other scientific use.'

Project licences are not to be granted authorising the use of cats, dogs, primates or equidae unless it can be established that other sorts of animals are either not suitable or impracticable to obtain. Additionally (unless the Secretary of State is prepared to make an exception) they must contain a condition to the effect that no cat or dog is to be used unless they have been bred or obtained from a designated breeding establishment. The criteria for these are set out in Section 7 (the same condition applies to animals listed in Schedule 2, ie mouse, rat, guinea pig, hamster, rabbit, dog, cat, primate).

The regulated procedure must be carried out in the place specified in the personal and project licences. Section 6 provides that no place may be specified in the licence unless it is a designated establishment, and a certificate has been issued to that effect by the Secretary of State. A certificate must not be issued except to a person '. . . occupying a position of authority at the establishment in question', and must specify

'(a) a person to be responsible for the day-to-day care of the protected animals kept for experimental or other scientific purposes at the establishment; and

(b) a veterinary surgeon or other suitably qualified person to provide advice on their health and welfare.'

Any certificate issued under the Section must contain a condition that the protected animals kept at the establishment for experimental or for other scientific purposes must not be killed except by a method approved under Schedule 1 or approved by the Secretary of State even if they are not subjected to regulated procedure or required to be killed by the provisions of Section 15.

Section 12 provides that the Secretary of State may revoke or vary any licence granted but before doing so a notice must be served on the holder who may within the specified period (which must not be less than 28 days) make representations. Section 13 provides for immediate suspension of a licence in cases of urgency but only for a maximum three month period.

7

There are other provisions in the Act designed to reduce suffering in animals used for experiments.

Section 14 deals with the issue of the 're-use' of animals; and Section 15 with the issue of humane killing at the end of the experiment.

Other provisions in the Act are as follows:

Section 16 prohibits the showing of regulated procedures to the general public as an exhibition or on the television or advertising any such showings; Section 17 bans the use of neuromuscular blocking agents in the course of regulated procedures unless same is expressly authorised by the personal and project licences. The use of any such agent instead of an anaesthetic is banned completely. Section 18 enables the Secretary of State to appoint inspectors to advise regarding certificates and licences and to visit premises; and Section 19 sets up the 'Animals Procedures Committee', which advises the Secretary of State regarding the operation of the Act, and '... shall have regard both to the legitimate requirements of science and industry and to the protection of animals against avoidable suffering and unnecessary use in scientific procedures'. At least two thirds of the committee's membership must have one of various stipulated qualifications, one of which is full registration as a medical practitioner.

It has already been mentioned that contravention of Section 3 is a criminal offence. The same applies to many other provisions. Additionally Section 24 provides for the criminal prosecution of anyone who wrongly discloses information obtained by him in the course of exercising his functions under the Act 'and which he knows or has reasonable grounds for believing to have been given in confidence'.

7.3.1 Medicinal Tests on Animals

In subchapter 3.8 we have set out the legal controls which exist relating to the import of drugs for use in medicinal tests on animals. These are set out in the Medicines Act 1968, and the same Act restricts the circumstances in which substances may be administered to animals in the course of such tests. It should be noted that these provisions are subject to the other laws set out here concerning cruelty.

The phrase 'medicinal tests on animals' is defined in Section 32(6) of the Act as being '. . . an investigation or series of investigations consisting of any of the following, that is to say -

(a) the administration of a medicinal product of a particular description to one or more animals, where there is evidence that medicinal products of that description have effects which may be beneficial to, or otherwise advantageous in relation to, that animal or those animals, and the product is administered for the purpose of ascertaining whether, or to what extent, it has those or any other effects, whether advantageous or otherwise;

(b) the administration of a medicinal product to one or more animals in circumstances where there is no such evidence as is mentioned in the preceding paragraph, and the product is administered for the purpose of ascertaining whether, or to what extent, it has any effects relevant to a medicinal purpose;

(c) the administration of any substance or article, other than a medicinal product, to one or more animals for the purpose of ascertaining whether it has any effects relevant to a medicinal purpose, whether there is evidence that it has effects which may be beneficial to, or otherwise advantageous in relation to, that animal or those animals or not.'

Section 132 provides that the term 'animal' includes any bird, fish or reptile.

The terms 'medicinal product' and 'medicinal purpose' are also defined (these definitions are set out in the glossary).

Section 32(4) of the Act prohibits the administration (or the procuring of the administration) of 'any substance or article' to an animal in the course of a medicinal test on animals by any person in the course of a business.

The term 'administered' is defined in Section 130(9) to include administration

'orally, by injection or by introduction into the body in any other way or by external application, whether by direct contact with the body or not'; and also included are circumstances where the substance has 'been dissolved or dispensed in, or diluted or mixed with, some other substance used as a vehicle'.

To this general prohibition there are some exemptions, but none of these apply specifically to doctors.

The first of these is set out in Section 33(1) and consists of two elements: where,

'the test is, or is to be, carried out in circumstances where there is no evidence that the substance or article has effects which may be beneficial to, or otherwise advantageous in relation to, the animal or animals to which it is, or is to be, administered', and

where there is no prospect of the carcass being eaten by humans.

If the 'substance' falls within the definition of 'medicinal product' then the test may be carried out if the experimenter holds a 'product licence' 'which authorises that test and the product is administered in accordance with that licence or in accordance with any instructions required by the licence to be communicated to the person carrying out the test'. (Section 32(4)(a).)

Section 32(5) defines a product licence for these purposes as

'. . . a licence which authorises a particular medicinal test on animals if -

(a) the substance or article to be administered in the test is a medicinal product of the description to which the licence relates, and

(b) the uses of medicinal products of that description which are referred to in the licence are such as to include their use for the purposes of that test.'

Whether or not the substance or article used falls within the definition of a medicinal product then the third exception to the prohibition is that where an 'animal test certificate' has been issued. Such certificates must certify that subject to the provisions of the certificate, the licensing authority have consented to the test in question'. (Section 32(2)(b).)

The certificate must also be 'for the time being in force and the substance or article is administered in accordance with that certificate'. (Section 32(4)(b).)

The Act sets out the provisions for obtaining licences and certificates.

The general effect of Section 32 can be modified by government order (see Section 35(8)(b).) Various orders have been made. (See Painter AA ed.

7

Butterworths Law of Food and Drugs, London: Butterworths, 1981, Section 170.)

7.3.2 Inhumane Operations

The Protection of Animals Act 1911 (not applicable in Scotland and Northern Ireland) and the Protection of Animals (Scotland) Act 1912 provide that it is a criminal offence to:

'. . . subject, or cause or procure, or being the owner permit, to be subjected, any animal to any operation which is performed without due care or humanity'.

The term 'animal' in this context is defined to include any domestic or captive animal, and those terms are defined as follows.

'Domestic animal' means 'any horse, ass, mule, bull, sheep, pig, goat, dog, cat or fowl, or any other animal of whatsoever kind or species, and whether a quadruped or not which is tame or which has been or is being sufficiently tamed to serve some purpose for the use of man.'

The term 'captive animal' means any animal 'of whatsoever kind or species, and whether a quadruped or not, including any bird, fish, or reptile, which is in captivity, or confinement, or which is maimed, pinioned, or subjected to any appliance or contrivance for the purpose of hindering or preventing its escape from captivity or confinement'.

This does not render illegal an operation sanctioned under the Cruelty to Animals Act 1876 or the Animals (Scientific Procedures) Act 1986 but, as already mentioned, medicinal tests on animals will be illegal if performed contrary to these provisions. Other exceptions relate to killing animals for food, unless unnecessary suffering is thereby caused, and the coursing or hunting of captive animals unless liberated in an injured, mutilated or exhausted condition.

It must be noted that the Protection of Animals (Anaesthetics) Act 1954 (not applicable in Northern Ireland) provides that an operation will, for these purposes, be assumed to have been performed without humanity if it is performed on an animal without the use of an anaesthetic to prevent pain during an operation. (Section 1(1).)

Section 1(2) provides that this proviso applies '. . . to any operation with or without the use of instruments which involves interference with the sensitive tissue or bone structure of an animal' except for '. . . the making of injections or extractions by means of a hollow needle'. Once again operations sanctioned by the Animals (Scientific Procedures Act) 1986 and certain docking, castration and other minor operations performed by veterinary surgeons are excepted.

7.3.3 Veterinary Surgery

The Veterinary Surgeons Act 1966 provides in Section 19 that it is a criminal offence for a person who is not a registered veterinary surgeon or practitioner to

7

practise or to hold himself out as practising veterinary surgery. There are some exceptions to this rule, some of which apply to doctors. These are as follows.

1   An experiment authorised under the Animal (Scientific Procedures) Act 1986.

2   'The performance by a registered medical practitioner of an operation on an animal for the purpose of removing an organ or tissue for use in the treatment of human beings'. (Section 19(4)(c).)

3   'The carrying out or performance of any treatment, test or operation by a registered medical practitioner or a registered dentist at the request of' a registered veterinary surgeon or practitioner. (Section 19(4)(d).)

Veterinary surgery is defined to include (Section 27):

'(a) the diagnosis of diseases in, and injuries to animals including tests performed on animals for diagnostic purposes;

(b) the giving of advice based on such diagnosis;

(c) the medical or surgical treatment of animals; and

(d) the performance of surgical operations on animals.'

The term 'animal' here includes birds and reptiles.

7.4   Anatomy

The Anatomy Act 1984 (not applicable in Northern Ireland) came into force in February 1988. It has replaced the Anatomy Acts of 1832 and 1871, and Section 2(1) and Section 3 of the Human Tissue Act 1961.

The 1984 Act regulates the performance of anatomical examinations and the possession of anatomical specimens and the later retention of same.

It should be noted that the Anatomy Act 1984 does not regulate the conduct of post mortem examinations nor the removal of parts of the body when such has been authorised under the provisions of Section 1 of the Human Tissue Act 1961 (see subchapter 1.3) for the purposes of medical education and research even if the latter involves anatomical examinations. In such a case the Human Tissue Act regulates the position although the Anatomy Act is not thereby prevented from applying after the removal of the tissue has taken place or if there is in the event no removal.

Section 2 of the Anatomy Act prohibits the performance of anatomical examinations and the possession of anatomical specimens unless certain criteria are met. Before considering the position in relation to anatomical examinations it is necessary to consider what is meant by this expression for the purposes of the Act. Section 1 defines an anatomical examination as follows:

'The examination by dissection of a body for purposes of teaching or studying, or researching into, morphology; and where parts of a body are separated in the course of its anatomical examination, such examination includes the examination by dissection of the parts for those purposes.'

Anatomical examinations may be carried out only if four conditions are satisfied, as follows:

1 Anatomical examinations must only be carried out on premises licensed under Section 3(1), which authorises the Secretary of State to issue such licences.

2 The person who carries out the examination must be authorised to do so under Section 3(3). Such authorisation may derive from a licence granted by the Secretary of State to that person or from the fact that the person '. . . carries out the examination in the course of teaching or studying, or researching into, morphology and has permission (general or particular) to carry out the examination from a person who is so licensed at the time of the examination.'

(See subchapter 7.4.2 for more about licences.)

3 The examination must be lawful according to the provisions of Section 4, which deals with the issue of who may authorise the use of the body for the purposes of anatomy. Thus the person who is 'lawfully in possession' (see below) may authorise an anatomical examination if the deceased '. . . either in writing at any time or orally in the presence of two or more witnesses during his last illness, has expressed a request that his body be used after his death for anatomical examination' (provided there is no reason to believe the request was withdrawn before death). Or if having made such reasonable inquiry as may be practicable that person has no reason to believe

'(a) that the deceased, either in writing or at any time orally in the presence of two or more witnesses during his last illness, had expressed an objection to his body being so used after his death, and had not withdrawn it, or

(b) that the surviving spouse or any surviving relative of the deceased objects to the body being so used.'

In those cases where the body is 'lawfully in the possession' of a hospital, nursing home or other institution the Act permits the managers to delegate the right to give authority for anatomical examination to a designated person. (Section 4(9).)

The subject of who is 'lawfully in possession' has already been discussed in subchapter 1.3.2. In the footnote to the Anatomy Act *Halsbury's Statutes of England and Wales* review the English authorities. They point out that in the case of Williams v. Williams 1882 20 ChD 659 [1881-5] AER rep 840, it was held that the executors have a right to possession of a corpse. The case of R v Feist [1858] Dears' B 590; 27 LJMC 164, however, decided that for the

7

purposes of Section 7 of the Anatomy Act 1832 (which has been replaced by the Anatomy Act 1984) where a person died in a workhouse the master of the workhouse was a 'party having lawful possession'. They also point out that the provision above in Subsection 9 implies that in the case of death in a hospital the manager thereof is in lawful possession. They state that the Canadian case Edmonds v Armstrong Funeral Home Ltd. [1931] 1 DLR 676 decided that there is a general right to possession in the surviving husband, wife or next of kin. (This case would be of what is termed persuasive authority only in this country, ie an English court would not have to follow the case but could be persuaded by it.) Halsbury's ends by stating that some assistance might be derived from the list of persons responsible for notifying a death under the Births and Deaths Registration Act 1953 (on this, see subchapter 8.4.1). It would appear that, as in the case of donation of tissue, the question of who is 'lawfully in possession' could in theory be open to debate, but in the majority of cases in practice this is improbable.

There are certain limitations on the right of the person 'lawfully in possession' to authorise an anatomical examination.

(a) In England and Wales if a person has reason to believe that an inquest may be required to be held or that a post mortem may be required by the coroner then that person must not without the consent of the coroner give or act on any authority to perform an anatomical examination.

In Scotland if a person has reason to believe that an inquiry under the Fatal Accidents and Sudden Deaths Inquiry (Scotland) Act 1976 is to be held or that a post mortem may be required by the procurator fiscal that person must not without the consent of the procurator fiscal give or act on any authority to perform an anatomical examination.

(b) No authority to perform an anatomical examination may be given by a person entrusted with a body only for the purposes of interment or cremation.

(c) Any authority given expires at the end of the statutory period even if the authority is expressed to be for a longer time. The Act states that the statutory period is three years from the death but power is given to the Secretary of State to vary the length of the period by order.

4　The last provision which must be complied with in relation to anatomical examinations is that the death must have been registered under Section 15 of the Births and Deaths Registration Act 1953 or in Scotland under Section 22 of the Births, Deaths and Marriages (Scotland) Act 1965.

A person who carries out an anatomical examination otherwise than as permitted under Section 2(1) can be prosecuted in the criminal courts. This is stated in Section 11.

Before considering the position in relation to possession of anatomical specimens it is necessary to consider how the Act defines same. The Act states in Section 1(2) that an anatomical specimen means for these purposes

'(a) a body to be used for anatomical examination, or

(b) a body in course of being used for anatomical examination (including separated parts of such a body).'

A 'body' means a 'body of a deceased person'.

Section 2 of the Act states that no one may possess an anatomical specimen unless the following criteria are satisfied.

1 The person in possession must be so authorised under Section 3(4). The authority can derive either from a licence granted by the Secretary of State or if the person has '. . . from a person who is so licensed at that time, permission (general or particular) to have such possession'. (See sub-chapter 7.4.2 for more details about licences.)

2 Anatomical examination of a specimen must at the time be properly authorised in accordance with the provisions of Section 4 (see above).

3 A certificate regarding the cause of death must be signed in accordance with Section 22(1) of the Births and Deaths Registration Act 1953 and Section 24 of the Births, Deaths and Marriages (Scotland) Act 1965. (These are the Sections requiring a medical certificate to be signed. The provisions are set out in subchapter 8.4.)

These restrictions do not apply to a person who comes into lawful possession of a body immediately after death and retains possession prior to the removal of the body to a place where the anatomical examination takes place. Otherwise a person who contravenes these provisions can be prosecuted in the criminal courts.

7.4.1 Subsequent Possession

Section 5 of the Act regulates the question of possession of a body or parts of a body in circumstances where an authority given under Section 4 (see above) has expired or where an anatomical examination has been concluded before such expiry. The general rule is that no one may in such circumstances possess the body or a part of the body unless they do so 'for the purpose only of its decent disposal' or if a list of other criteria are satisfied which are as follows.

1 The person must be in possession of a part of a body concerning which an anatomical examination has been concluded and before the expiry of an authority given as per Section 4 (see above).

2 The part of the body must be such that the person from whose body it came could not be recognised simply by examination of the part.

3 The person in possession must have been authorised in accordance with

Section 5(5). Under this Subsection the Secretary of State may license possession '. . . in the interests of education or research' of parts of bodies or a person may be authorised by permission granted by the person with the licence.

4   The possession of the part must be authorised by the person 'lawfully in possession' of the body in accordance with the provisions of Section 6. These provisions are phrased the same as those under Section 4 (above), ie the person in possession can authorise retention of a part of a body if the deceased has requested this or there is no reason to believe that he would have objected or that his relatives now object.

It is a criminal offence to retain a body or part of one in contravention of these provisions.

7.4.2 Licences

Section 7.4 sets out the general provisions about licences under the Anatomy Act. These may be granted to such persons as the Secretary of State considers to be suitable. If a licence is refused the applicant is to be notified in writing of the refusal and the reasons for it. In certain circumstances the Secretary of State can attach conditions to the licence but not in relation to matters covered by Regulations laid down under Section 8 (see below). The licence can be revoked and ends on the death of the licensee. Any permissions that can be given by the licence holder terminate 21 days after the death of the licence holder (or earlier if so specified).

Under Section 8 regulations may be made with a view to securing efficient and orderly examinations and the decent disposal of the bodies (and parts of them) after their examination has been concluded and to ensure that parts of bodies retained are to be decently cared for.

Under Section 3 licensed persons must keep such records as may be required by regulations and retain these for such period as is specified.

Lastly the Act provides in Section 9 for the appointment of Inspectors of Anatomy to, amongst other things, inspect premises and consider licence applications. Section 10 sets out the rights for such inspectors to inspect records and premises.

8 Birth and Death

In section 9.4.2 it is stated that legal controls exist over who may lawfully attend midwives. As a result of attending at a birth, however, doctors may find themselves under various legal duties. Some of these duties arise by virtue of mere presence but in one case, that of stillbirths, the doctor by virtue of being a doctor is placed under a special obligation.

8.1 Duties to Notify and Register Births

8.1.1 Duty to Notify Birth to Health Authorities

In England and Wales the National Health Service Act 1977 provides a duty of notification when a birth takes place.

The duty is imposed on the father of every child born if he is residing on the premises where the birth takes place and on any person in attendance on the mother at the time of or within six hours after the birth.

The duty applies to notify regarding any child which has issued forth from its mother after the expiry of the 28th week of pregnancy whether alive or dead.

The duty is to give notice of the birth to the prescribed medical officer (ie prescribed in National Health Service (Notification of Births and Deaths) Regulations 1982 (S.I. 1982 No.286) or to the District Health Authority for the place where the birth takes place. The notice must be given either by posting or delivering same within 36 hours after the birth. Failure to do so is a criminal offence unless the accused can satisfy the court that he believed some other person had done so.

The District Health Authority must supply without charge pre-paid stamped addressed envelopes together with forms of notice to any medical practitioner or midwife residing or practising in their area who applies to them for same. (Section 124, as amended.)

In Scotland the Registrar sends details of the child's birth to the local area Health Board but there is no equivalent to Section 124 in the National Health Service (Scotland) Act 1978.

8

8.1.2 The Duty to Give Particulars of Live Births (and Stillbirths) to the Registrar of Births and Deaths

The law about this is set out in England and Wales in the Births and Deaths Registration Act 1953, Section 2, and in Scotland in the Registration of Births, Deaths and Marriages (Scotland) Act 1965, Section 14.

In the case of every birth there is a duty to notify same to the Registrar. This duty falls primarily on the mother and father but in the event of their death or inability the duty then falls on any other qualified informant (see below).

The duty is as follows. The informant must within 42 days in England and Wales and 21 days in Scotland provide the Registrar with all the required information concerning the birth and sign the register in the presence of the Registrar. The required information is set out in the Schedule to the Population (Statistics) Act 1938 as substituted by the Population (Statistics) Act 1960.

Once one qualified informant has done this then all the others are relieved of any such duty.

In England and Wales if, before the 42 days are up, an inquest has found that the child was stillborn the duty to notify the birth no longer applies.

The above Acts provide that certain categories of persons are qualified to give information about births. They may be referred to as 'qualified informants'. The categories are:

(a) The father and mother of the child.

(b) The occupier of a house where to the knowledge of that occupier a child has been born.

(c) Any person present at the birth.

(d) Any person having charge of the child.

If the required particulars have not been provided within the respective time limits then the Registrar is empowered by virtue of Section 4 (England and Wales) and Section 16 (Scotland) to serve a notice on the person who is a qualified informant requiring him to attend personally at the Registrar's office to give necessary details of the birth. It should be noted that by Section 36(a) (England and Wales) and Section 53(3) (Scotland) a person who is required by the statutes to give information concerning a birth and who 'wilfully refuses to answer any questions put to him' by the Registrar relating to the particulars required to be registered concerning the birth or fails to comply with any requirement made by the Registrar in accordance with the statutes can be prosecuted and fined in the criminal courts.

Section 8 (England and Wales) and Section 17 (Scotland) forbid registration of a birth after three months have elapsed unless additional special procedures are followed.

8.2   Duties in Relation to Stillbirths

The same Acts also govern the legal position regarding notification of stillbirths to the registrar. Section 41 is the Interpretation section of the Births and Deaths Registration Act 1953: this states that a 'stillborn child means a child which has issued forth from its mother after the twenty-eighth week of pregnancy and which did not at any time after being completely expelled from its mother breathe, or show any other signs of life, and the expression "stillbirth" shall be construed accordingly'.

Under Section 11(1) (England and Wales) and Section 21 (Scotland) every registered medical practitioner or certified midwife who has been present at a stillbirth or who examines the body of a stillborn child must on being requested by a qualified informant (see above) give that informant a certificate in the prescribed form. For the form prescribed in England and Wales see the Registration of Births, Deaths and Marriages Regulations (S.I. 1987 No.2088).

The certificate must state that the child was not born alive and where possible must state to the best of the knowledge and belief of the person signing it the cause of death. The certificate must also state in England and Wales the estimated duration of the pregnancy and in Scotland such particulars of the condition of the mother before the stillbirth as may be requested in the prescribed form.

The qualified informant must then produce the certificate to the Registrar and it is stipulated that the certificate should be requested from the doctor in preference to the midwife if there is a choice of both. If there is no doctor or midwife eligible to sign a certificate then the qualified informant must sign a declaration to that effect.

See under Death Certificates, subchapter 8.4.1, for the sanctions which operate if a doctor neglects to provide a certificate when under a duty to do so under these Acts or if a certificate is provided which contains false or inaccurate particulars.

8.3   Doctors and Inquiries into a Death

8.3.1   Doctors and Coroners: England and Wales

In this chapter the following issues are considered.

Does a doctor by virtue of being a doctor owe any duty to report the fact of a death to a coroner? Is there any other duty to do so? Is there a duty by virtue of being a doctor to report the fact of a death to any other official who in turn might report the death to the coroner?

What circumstances relevant to doctors might lead that other official to report the fact of the death to the coroner?

What powers does the coroner have to summon medical witnesses to post mortems?

8

There is no general statutory duty imposed on the doctor by virtue of being a doctor to report a death to the coroner but it is accepted practice for him to do so in cases of doubt and suspicion. Such cases would generally include:

Sudden death where the cause is unclear where there was non-attendance in the last illness;

Accidents in any way contributing to the cause of death;

Chronic or acute alcoholism contributing to the death;

Death where an anaesthetic or surgical procedure appears to have contributed to the death or where an operation was performed following an injury;

Drug related death whether therapeutic or otherwise;

Death of a foster child;

Death that may be related to any industrial disease;

Death where the deceased has been in receipt of a disability pension;

Deaths related to any forms of poisoning whether deliberate or unintentional;

Stillbirths where there was any possibility of the child being born alive.

Obstruction of the coroner is also a common law offence but the prosecution must prove that the defendant disposed of the body with intent to obstruct or prevent a coroner's inquest in circumstances where there would have been a duty to hold same. (R v Pearson, 1954, unreported.)

Section 3(1) of the Coroners' Act 1887 states that the coroner must hold an inquest when he '. . . is informed that the dead body of a person is lying within his jurisdiction, and there is reasonable cause to suspect that such person has died either a violent or an unnatural death, or has died a sudden death of which the cause is unknown, or that such person has died in prison, or in such place or under such circumstances as to require an inquest in pursuance of any Act'.

The coroner is permitted to dispense with an inquest in a case of sudden death where the cause of death is unknown, if he orders a post mortem and is satisfied by the outcome that death was due to natural causes. The coroner notifies the Registrar by completing Pink Form B. This is the lower half of a composite form; the upper half of which – Pink Form A – permits the cause of death given on the doctor's death certificate to be registered, ie in cases of death from natural causes.

Although doctors are not under a statutory duty to report any death to the coroner they are obliged in certain circumstances to sign a death certificate and deliver same to the Registrar of Births and Deaths. See subchapter 8.4 for details of this duty and the duty of all persons in certain circumstances to report the fact of the death to the Registrar.

The Registrar in turn is under a statutory duty to inform the coroner of the fact of the death in certain circumstances, some of which directly relate to medical treatment or the lack of it.

The Registration of Births, Deaths and Marriages Regulations (S.I. 1987 No.2088) state firstly (Regulation 33), that where the Registrar is informed of a stillbirth and has reason to believe that the child was born alive he must report that matter to the coroner.

Secondly, Regulation 71 states that if a registrar is told of a death within twelve months of its occurrence the fact of the death must be reported to the coroner if the death is one:

'(a) in respect of which the deceased was not attended during his last illness by a registered medical practitioner; or

(b) in respect of which the registrar

    i has been unable to obtain a duly completed certificate of cause of death; or

    ii has received such a certificate with respect to which it appears to him, from the particulars contained in the certificate or otherwise, that the deceased was seen by the certifying medical practitioner neither after death or within fourteen days before death; or

(c) the cause of which appears to be unknown; or

(d) which the registrar has reason to believe to have been unnatural or to have been caused by violence or neglect or by abortion or to have been attended by suspicious circumstances; or

(e) which appears to the registrar to have occurred during an operation or before recovery from the effect of an anaesthetic; or

(f) which appears to the registrar from the contents of any medical certificate to have been due to industrial disease or industrial poisoning.'

Note too that Rule 19 of the Prison Rules (S.I. 1964 No.388) obliges prison governors to notify the coroner of any death in prison and a similar duty is imposed in relation to inmates of youth custody and detention centres.

8

A coroner may of course in practice be notified of a death by the police or by the coroner's officers.

Statute provides that medical witnesses can be summoned to give evidence at inquests and medical practitioners can be ordered to perform post mortems. Those who disobey can be penalised.

Section 21 of the Coroners' Act 1887 enables the coroner to summon the doctor who last treated the deceased, or, if there were none, another doctor practising in the area where the death occurred.

'Where it appears to the coroner that the deceased was attended at his death or during his last illness by any legally qualified medical practitioner, the coroner may summon such practitioner as a witness; but if it appears to the coroner that the deceased person was not attended at his death or during his last illness by any legally qualified medical practitioner, the coroner may summon any legally qualified medical practitioner who is at the time in actual practice in or near the place where the death happened, and any such medical witness as is summoned in pursuance of this section, may be asked to give evidence as to how, in his opinion, the deceased came to his death.'

The person so summoned can be directed also to perform a post mortem but note the provisions below which in effect direct a coroner, if possible, only to select a doctor with suitable qualifications to perform post mortems.

Also if there is any allegation of negligence against a doctor that doctor should not be asked to perform a post mortem.

'Provided that where a person states upon oath before the coroner that in his belief the death of the deceased was caused partly or entirely by the improper or negligent treatment of a medical practitioner or other person, such medical practitioner or other person shall not be allowed to perform or assist at the post-mortem·examination of the deceased.' (Section 21(2).)

In addition, if a coroner receives a written request from an inquest jury requesting that another medical practitioner named by them should be summoned and further directed to perform a post mortem even if one has already been done the coroner must comply with that request. (Section 21(3).) The jury may make such a request if they '. . . are of the opinion that the cause of death has not been satisfactorily explained by the evidence of the medical practitioner or other witnesses brought before them'.

Section 23 of the Coroners' Act 1887 states that any medical practitioner who fails to obey a summons of the coroner issued in pursuance of that Act can be prosecuted and fined unless he can show good and sufficient cause for such disobedience.

8

The Coroners' (Amendment) Act 1926 (as amended) sets out additional powers in relation to the summoning of medical witnesses. Section 22 states that in addition to the powers set out above a coroner may at any time after he has decided to hold an inquest require any legally qualified medical practitioner to hold a post mortem examination or examination of parts of the body or other relevant substances or things. There is the same caveat as above against making such a request to a doctor against whom there has been made an allegation of negligence on oath but there is an additional right given to the person against whom such an allegation has been made if he so wishes to be 'represented' at the post mortem. (Section 22(4).)

The Coroners Rules (S.I. 1984 No.552) Rule 6, direct a coroner to have regard to certain criteria when considering which medical practitioner to request to perform a post mortem. Firstly the post mortem '. . . should be made, whenever practicable, by a pathologist with suitable qualifications and experience and having access to laboratory facilities'. If it seems likely that someone is to be charged with murder the coroner should consult with the police as to who should be asked to do the post mortem. If the deceased died in hospital the coroner should not appoint a pathologist on the staff of or associated with that hospital to do the post mortem if certain criteria apply, nor should a doctor who is on a pneumoconiosis medical panel be asked to do so if the disease is in the category dealt with by that panel.

8.3.2 Doctors and the Procurator Fiscal: Scotland

There is no office of coroner in Scotland. In Scotland the procurator fiscal is charged with inquiring into all sudden suspicious, accidental, unexpected and unexplained deaths, ie:

1 Any uncertain death.

2 Any death which was caused by an accident arising out of the use of a vehicle, or which was caused by an aircraft or rail accident.

3 Any death arising out of industrial employment, by accident, industrial disease or industrial poisoning.

4 Any death due to poisoning (coal gas, barbiturate, etc).

5 Any death where the circumstances would seem to indicate suicide.

6 Any death where there are indications that it occurred under an anaesthetic.

7 Any death resulting from an accident in the home, hospital, institution or any public place.

8 Any death following an abortion.

9 Any death apparently caused by neglect (eg malnutrition).

10 Any death occurring in prison or a police cell where deceased was in custody at the time of death.

11 Any death of a newborn child whose body is found.

12 Any death (occurring not in a house) where deceased's residence is unknown.

13 Death by drowning.

14 Death of a child from suffocation (including overlaying).

15 Where the death occurred as the result of smallpox or typhoid.

16 Any death as a result of a fire or explosion.

17 Any sudden death.

8

18 Any other death due to violent, suspicious or unexplained cause.

19 Deaths of foster children.

The procurator fiscal is required in terms of the Fatal Accidents and Sudden Deaths Inquiry (Scotland) Act 1976 to hold a Public Inquiry before the Sheriff in the circumstances set out in Section 1 which include, for example, all deaths in the course of employment or while in custody or where it is considered expedient to do so on grounds that the death was sudden, suspicious or unexplained or gave rise to serious public concern and the procurator fiscal must, in addition, report to the Crown Office deaths occurring in a range of specified circumstances.

Such an inquiry is held in public and the proceedings are transcribed in shorthand. A doctor can be compelled to attend and give a precognition to the procurator fiscal and subsequently can be compelled to give evidence at the inquiry and must answer all the questions (save those which might point to his being guilty of a criminal offence). The Sheriff then issues a determination covering such matters as place and cause of death, the defects in any system of work resulting in death and the reasonable precautions by which death might have been avoided. It can be seen that any doctor who is involved in the circumstances which led up to the death and who is at any risk, however slight or far-reached, should have legal representation at the inquiry and even lead witnesses of his own. The transcript of the evidence at the inquiry can be used and referred to in subsequent civil proceedings.

It is worth bearing in mind that the procurator fiscal is only obliged to instruct a post mortem if he considers the circumstances justified. Accordingly, if a doctor, following upon a death of a patient, considers that his treatment or diagnosis or any action is liable to be criticised then it may be advisable for him to demand a post mortem in order that the precise cause of death is established from the beginning.

There is no general statutory duty in Scotland on a doctor to report to the procurator fiscal a death falling within the categories into which the latter must inquire although clearly as a matter of public duty, any citizen and particularly a medically qualified one should report such deaths. It is doubtful whether failure to do so would be a breach of any general common law obligation.

The Registrar of Births, Marriages and Deaths is, however, statutorily obliged to inform the procurator fiscal of all deaths into which the procurator fiscal must inquire (Registration of Births, Deaths and Marriages (Scotland) Act 1965). A medical practitioner who attended the deceased in his last illness must, within seven days of death, send either to the Registrar or to any person who has an obligation to inform the Registrar (ie any relative of the deceased, any person present at the death, the deceased's executor or legal representative, the occupier of the premises where the deceased died) a certificate of prescribed form stating the cause of death. If no doctor was attendant during the final illness or if the doctor present at the death cannot provide the certificate, then

8

any medical practitioner who is able to do so may sign (Section 24). (This is different from the position in England, where only the coroner or doctor in attendance during the last illness can sign the certificate.) If the doctor feels unable to sign the certificate he should contact the procurator fiscal and if the latter is satisfied that no crime or matter which might involve him are concerned he will say so and the doctor can sign the certificate.

8.4 Death Certificates and Notification

Another point that should be noted is that a doctor who signs a certificate containing a statement that later turns out to be untrue, misleading or otherwise improper renders himself liable to disciplinary proceedings. (See GMC blue booklet April 1987, para 45.)

In addition many statutes which provide for the signing of medical certificates also provide for the prosecution in the criminal courts of anyone who signs such a certificate with a false statement in it.

8.4.1 Death Certificates

See subchapter 9.4 for further points concerning certificates. Details of the duty to give a certificate where a stillbirth has occurred are set out in subchapter 8.2. In addition in England and Wales the Births and Deaths Registration Act 1953 and in Scotland the Registration of Births, Deaths and Marriages (Scotland) Act 1965 provide that if a patient has been attended during his last illness by a registered medical practitioner then that doctor must sign a death certificate.

In England and Wales Section 22(1) of the Act provides that the certificate must be in the form prescribed by the Registration of Births, Deaths and Marriages Regulations (S.I. 1987 No.2088) Forms 14 and 15. The latter form applies when death occurs within 28 days of birth. This now includes amongst other things a requirement to certify if death might have been due or contributed to by the employment of the deceased. The certificate must also contain a statement by the doctor as to the cause of death to the best of his knowledge and belief. If the doctor cannot do so then there is no obligation to sign the death certificate.

Having signed the certificate the registered medical practitioner must deliver same forthwith to the Registrar of Births and Deaths. The doctor must also give to a 'qualified informant' (see below) notice in writing in the form prescribed by the Registration of Births, Deaths and Marriages Regulations (S.I. 1987 No.2088) Form 16. That informant must, except where an inquest is held, deliver this notice to the Registrar.

In Scotland Section 24 provides that the registered medical practitioner must deliver the certificate either to a qualified informant (see later) or to the Registrar within seven days or such period as is prescribed by Regulations (the minimum period which can be prescribed is two days). This section also

8

provides that if there is no registered medical practitioner available who is eligible or able to sign a certificate then such a certificate may be signed by any medical practitioner who is able to do so.

Both Acts provide that a person who is required by virtue of the legislation to give, deliver or send any certificate who fails to do so without reasonable excuse is guilty of an offence. (See Section 36(b) of the English statute and Section 53(3)(b) of the Scottish statute.)

8.4.2 Registration of Death

There is a statutory duty under the legislation referred to above to notify the Registrar of the fact that a death has occurred. In England and Wales persons who can be obliged to report the death (referred to as 'qualified informants') are as follows.

(a) Those under the primary duty are any relatives who were present at the death or who attended the deceased in his last illness or who live or were in the sub-district where the death occurred.

(b) Secondly the duty falls on any person present at the death or occupier of the house where it took place if he knew of it.

(c) Lastly the duty falls on any inmate of the house who knew of the death or person responsible for the disposal of the body.

Note that if the person died in a place other than a house, or if a body is found and no information is available about the place of death, then there is a similar duty imposed as follows.

(a) Firstly on any relative with knowledge of the particulars that have to be registered.

(b) Secondly any person present at the death.

(c) Thirdly any person finding or taking charge of the body.

(d) Lastly any person causing the disposal of the body.

In Scotland those with a duty to report the death are any of the following.

(a) Any relative of the deceased.

(b) Any person present at the death.

(c) The deceased's executor or other legal representative.

(d) The current occupier of the premises where the death took place.

(e) If none of the above, any other person with knowledge of the particulars that have to be registered.

8.5 Cremation Certificates

8.5.1 England and Wales

A cremation cannot take place unless a certificate has been signed by a registered medical practitioner. The law is set out in the Cremation Acts 1902 and 1952 and in various Regulations.

Section 8(2) of the 1902 Act provides that any person '. . . who shall wilfully make any false . . . representation, or sign or utter any false certificate, with a view to procuring the burning of any human remains' can be prosecuted and could receive up to two years' imprisonment.

In England and Wales the Cremation Regulations S.R. and O. 1930 No.1016 as amended provide the following.

Regulation 8 states that no cremation may take place unless one of five criteria has been satisfied and the Medical Referee has given his written authority (which he can refuse to do without giving a reason). The medical referee is a doctor attached to the cremation authority who must have not less than five years' standing and relevant experience and qualifications.

The criteria are either:

1   A certificate in the prescribed form must have been signed by a fully registered medical practitioner who must have attended the deceased during his last illness and must be able to certify definitely as to the cause of death. (Note the requirement that the doctor must certify 'definitely': as opposed to the best of his knowledge and belief, as with a death certificate.) The form of certificate is set out in Form B to the Schedule to the Regulations and it should be noted that more information is required than for a certificate under the Births, Deaths and Marriages Regulations.

    A confirmatory certificate in the form prescribed (ie as in Form C, set out in the Schedule) must be given by another registered medical practitioner who must be either the medical referee or another registered medical practitioner of five years' standing who must not be related to the deceased or related to or a partner of the doctor who gave the other certificate.

    A confirmatory certificate is not needed though if the person died in a hospital where he was an in-patient and a post mortem was performed by a doctor qualified as above and the registered medical practitioner who gave the Form B certificate knows the result of that examination before signing the certificate, or

2   A post mortem examination must have been carried out by a medical practitioner expert in pathology appointed by the cremation authority (or the medical referee in an emergency) and a certificate must have been given by him in the form set out in Form D in the Schedule, or

3   A post mortem must have been performed and the cause of death certified by the coroner and a certificate given by the coroner accordingly, or

4   An inquest must have been opened and a certificate given by the coroner, or

5   If the deceased has undergone anatomical examination then the person licensed under the relevant legislation must have given the necessary certificate.

The medical referee may permit the cremation of the remains of a stillborn child if the child has been certified to be stillborn by a registered medical practitioner after examination of the body and the medical referee is satisfied after making any necessary enquiries that the child was stillborn. But the medical referee must still get either a certificate of registration of the death or a certificate from the coroner regarding any inquest held. See Birth and Death, subchapter 8.1, for details of medical certificates given under these circumstances.

The BMA booklet *Deaths in the Community* prepared by the BMA's Forensic Medicine Subcommittee in 1986 gives guidance on the eight forms, ie Forms A,B,C,D,E,F,G and H, which must be completed for different aspects of cremation under the Cremation Act Regulations (as amended in 1985). The booklet reflects the situation in England and Wales relating to medical certification, notification to the coroner, interference with the body, stillbirths, the coroner's role and duties, together with disposal of the dead.

8.5.2   *Cremation in Scotland*

Before cremation can take place, a certificate must be signed by the doctor who attended the deceased during his last illness and who can definitely certify the cause of death. A confirmatory certificate by a doctor of five years' standing must also be given, except where the death took place while an in-patient in hospital and if a post mortem has taken place. (See for details – The Cremation (Amendment) (Scotland) Regulations (S.I. 1985 No.820).) If the certificate is not obtainable then a post mortem is carried out by an expert pathologist appointed by the cremation authority, and the procurator fiscal has to be informed of any suspicious circumstances or if there is reason to suspect that the death occurred under anaesthetic or if there are any suspicious circumstances surrounding a stillbirth. In general terms, if there is any doubt of the cause of death, the procurator fiscal should order a post mortem particularly where a cremation is envisaged.

8

9 Registered Medical Practitioners

9.1 Registration of Doctors

The statute currently governing the registration of medical practitioners is the Medical Act 1983. Under Section 2 of this Act the GMC is obliged to keep two registers of medical practitioners. Firstly, the 'register of medical practitioners' which is to contain four lists as follows.

(a) 'The principal list'. This contains the names of all doctors entitled to be fully or provisionally registered (see below) by virtue of UK or EEC qualifications or who have been directed to be registered by virtue of other foreign qualifications. Not included though are those who are entitled to be included in the overseas list.

(b) 'The overseas list'. This contains the names of those qualified as above but who are entitled by reason of residence outside the EEC to go on this list instead.

(c) 'The visiting overseas doctors list'. Under Section 27 temporary full registration may be granted to visiting overseas specialists if certain criteria apply for a period not exceeding 12 months.

(d) 'The visiting EEC practitioners list'. Under Section 18 an EEC national who is lawfully established in an EEC country in medical practice may be permitted to render medical services temporarily in the UK provided various criteria are met. This temporary registration ends if the doctor becomes established in medical practice in the UK or if (except in urgent cases) the doctor gives treatment outside the stated criteria.

Secondly the GMC must keep a register of medical practitioners with 'limited registration' (see below).

9.1.1 Full Registration

9.1.1.1 UK Doctors

Section 3(a) of the Act provides that the following are entitled to be fully registered. That is a person who:

1 Holds one or more primary United Kingdom qualifications. These are defined in Section 4(3) and include:

'(a) the degree of bachelor of medicine or bachelor of surgery granted by any university in the United Kingdom;

(b) licentiate of the Royal College of Physicians of London or the Royal College of Physicians of Edinburgh or the Royal College of Surgeons of Edinburgh or the Royal College (formally Royal Faculty) of Physicians and Surgeons of Glasgow;

(c) membership of the Royal College of Surgeons of England;

(d) licentiate in medicine and surgery of the Society of Apothecaries of London.'

2 Has passed a qualifying examination. Section 4(2) sets out the bodies who may hold same, and

3 Has obtained the necessary experience. Under Section 10 this involves being employed for the prescribed period in a resident medical capacity in one or more approved hospitals or institutions. A certificate verifying that the necessary experience has been obtained must be applied for and one will not be given unless the doctor has been employed in at least two prescribed branches of medicine for the minimum prescribed period such as to give the doctor the required experience. The doctor's service must additionally have been 'satisfactory'. (See below for details of provisional registration which enables doctors to obtain the necessary expertise.)

9.1.1.2   *EEC Doctors*

By virtue of Section 3(b) EEC doctors are entitled to be fully registered if they hold one or more primary European qualifications. (Defined in Section 17.)

9.1.1.3   *Other Overseas Doctors*

If the GMC sees fit so to direct, other overseas doctors may be fully registered if they can satisfy the Registrar of the following.

(a) That they hold one or more 'recognised overseas qualifications' (defined in Section 19(2)); and

(b) that they have the necessary knowledge of English, and that they are of good character; and

(c) that they have the necessary experience. Under Section 20 this means doing the same pre-registration house jobs as UK doctors or at least the equivalent abroad.

9.1.2 *Provisional Registration*

9.1.2.1   *UK Doctors*

Section 15 provides for provisional registration so that those wishing to obtain certificates of experience (see above para 9.1.1.1) can be employed to that end.

If a doctor would be entitled to full registration under Section 3(a) (see above) were it not for the fact that he has not yet obtained the necessary experience the doctor may be provisionally registered. This operates as full registration '. . . so far as is necessary to enable him to be engaged in employment in a resident medical capacity' in an approved hospital or institution but not further.

9.1.2.2 Other Overseas Doctors

Other overseas doctors may similarly be provisionally registered if they satisfy all the criteria necessary for full registration under Section 19 except the experience requirement. The effect of such registration is as above.

9.1.2.3 Limited Registration of Practitioners with Overseas Qualifications

Under Section 22 of the Act the criteria for limited registration are as follows. The person must:

(a) Have '. . . been selected for employment in the United Kingdom or the Isle of Man as a medical practitioner in one or more hospitals or other institutions approved by the General Medical Council'.

(b) Have '. . . passed the examination necessary for obtaining some acceptable overseas qualification'. (Defined in Section 22(4).)

(c) Have '. . . the necessary knowledge of English'.

(d) Be '. . . of good character'; and

(e) '. . . be someone who has the knowledge and skill, and has acquired the experience, which is necessary for practice as a medical practitioner registered under this section and is appropriate in his case'.

A person who satisfies the above criteria may be given limited registration if the GMC sees fit so to direct. Such registration cannot last longer than the specified period of time (which must not exceed five years in the aggregate) and may be granted either to cover a range of certain types of employment or in respect only of a particular appointment. If registration has been granted only for a particular appointment and the appointment ends earlier than expected then the registration ends also even if the specified period was for a longer period of time. Limited registration operates as full registration under Section 19 in relation to:

'(a) any employment in which he is engaged during the currency of his registration, being the particular employment or employment of a description for the purposes of which he is registered; and

(b) things done or omitted in the course of that employment; and

(c) any other thing incidental to his work in that employment which, by virtue of any enactment, may not lawfully or validly be done except by a fully registered medical practitioner;

9

but in relation to other matters he shall be treated as not so registered'.

Also note that doctors with limited registration must work under the supervision of a fully registered medical practitioner.

Section 25 of the Medical Act 1983 provides that a doctor who has held limited registration may proceed to full registration if he fulfils the GMC's requirements for so doing.

9.1.3 The Effect of Disciplinary Proceedings on Registration

Disciplinary proceedings could result in a doctor's name being erased from the register or in suspension from registration or in the registration being permitted to continue only on conditions.

Under Section 36 of the Act a doctor who is fully or provisionally registered or who has limited registration and who has been found guilty of a criminal offence or is judged by the Professional Conduct Committee of the GMC to have been guilty of serious professional misconduct may suffer the following penalties.

1 Erasure of name from the register. (The doctor can apply for restoration at a later date after at least 10 months.)

2 Suspension of registration. The doctor is treated as not being registered while the suspension operates. The suspension cannot exceed 12 months to start with. The period can be extended by further periods not exceeding 12 months each. Suspension could alternatively be followed by erasure or conditional registration as below.

3 Conditional registration for a period not exceeding three years '. . . with such requirements so specified as the Committee think fit to impose for the protection of members of the public or in his [that is the doctor's] interests'. See GMC blue booklet (paras 25-26) for examples of likely conditions. If the doctor fails to keep to the conditions his name can be erased or registration can be suspended (see above). The period of conditional registration can be extended by periods not exceeding 12 months each.

Additionally under Section 37, if the fitness to practise of any doctor, whether fully or provisionally registered or with limited registration, '. . . is judged by the Health Committee to be seriously impaired by reason of his physical or mental condition' then the Committee may direct suspension of registration or conditional registration as above. (See GMC blue booklet paras 112–118.)

Doctors may appeal against directions for erasure, suspension or conditional registration but Section 38(1) provides that the Professional Conduct and Health Committees have the power to order immediate suspension pending appeal if the decision was erasure or suspension '. . . if satisfied that to do so is necessary for the protection of members of the public or would be in the best interests of that person' [that is, the doctor].

9

For the criminal offence of pretending to be a registered medical practitioner see 9.2.1 below.

9.2 Privileges and Functions Reserved to Registered Medical Practitioners

There is no rule of law prohibiting non-registered persons from practising medicine but certain privileges and functions can only be enjoyed or performed by registered medical practitioners.

9.2.1 Rights to Use Titles

It is a criminal offence wilfully and falsely to pretend that one is a registered medical practitioner when in fact one is not. Section 49 of the Medical Act 1983 states that the offence is committed by a person who '. . . wilfully and falsely pretends to be or takes or uses the name or title of physician, doctor of medicine, licentiate in medicine and surgery, bachelor of medicine, surgeon, general practitioner or apothecary, or any name, title, addition or description implying that he is registered under any provision of this Act, or that he is recognised by law as a physician or surgeon or licentiate in medicine and surgery or a practitioner in medicine or an apothecary'.

9.2.2 Right to Recover Fees

Section 46 of the Medical Act 1983 reserves certain rights to sue for medical fees to fully registered medical practitioners only. The section states: 'no person shall be entitled to recover any charge in any court of law for any medical advice or attendance, or for the performance of any operation, or for any medicine which he has both prescribed and supplied unless he proves that he is fully registered'. This is subject to an exception for visiting EEC practitioners (see subchapter 9.1, Registration of Doctors, for definition of same).

9.2.3 Appointments Reserved for Fully Registered Medical Practitioners

Section 47 of the Medical Act 1983 provides that only a fully registered medical practitioner may hold an appointment as physician, surgeon or other medical officer in the following context:

'(a) in the naval, military or air services,

(b) in any hospital or other place for the reception of persons suffering from mental disorder, or in any other hospital, infirmary or dispensary not supported wholly by voluntary contributions,

(c) in any prison, or

(d) in any other public establishment, body or institution,

9

or to any friendly or other society for providing mutual relief in sickness, infirmity or old age.'

There is an exception to the above whereby a doctor who is not a Commonwealth citizen may act as the resident physician or medical officer of any hospital established exclusively for the relief of foreigners in sickness if various criteria are met.

Under the Health and Safety at Work etc. Act 1974, Section 56(2), no person is qualified to be appointed or to be an employment medical adviser unless he is a fully registered medical practitioner.

The National Health Service is also precluded from employing non-registered doctors. See National Health Service Act 1977 and National Health Service (General Medical and Pharmaceutical Services) Regulations (S.I. 1974 No.160) (as amended) and National Health Service (Scotland) Act 1978.

9.3 Jury Service

The relevant legislation is the Juries Act 1974 (England and Wales only) and the Law Reform (Miscellaneous Provisions) (Scotland) Act 1980. All persons between the ages of 18 and 65 who are registered to vote and who satisfy the necessary residence requirements are qualified and liable to serve on a jury unless they are 'ineligible' or 'disqualified'. Doctors as such are not included in either category but some doctors are entitled as of right to be excused from jury service if they so wish. Those with this right are medical practitioners who are registered (this includes those who are provisionally registered or registered with limited registration) and who are actually practising their profession. Also excused if they fulfil the same criteria are dentists, nurses, midwives, veterinary surgeons, and pharmaceutical chemists. A doctor may also be excused on the same basis if summoned to sit on a coroner's jury (not applicable in Scotland). Persons 'ineligible' to serve on a jury are firstly anyone who has ever (during the last 10 years in Scotland) been a member of the judiciary. That category includes JPs, chairmen, vice chairmen, presidents, vice presidents, registrars and assistant registrars of any tribunal. Secondly ineligible are persons who during the last ten years (five in Scotland) have been concerned in the administration of justice. This category includes medical officers and members of boards of visitors to penal establishments, members of the Parole Board and local review committees and in England and Wales only deputy, assistant and actual coroners and persons in charge of or employed in any forensic laboratory. Also ineligible are some mentally ill persons. People with serious criminal records are 'disqualified' from jury service.

A doctor who decides to do jury service must attend for as many days as he may be directed and is liable to serve on any jury at the place to which he is summoned. The legislation provides that a juror is entitled to certain allowances for travelling, subsistence and financial loss which may have occurred through eg loss of earnings. The amount allowed is fixed by prescribed rates which change from time to time.

9.4 Medical Certificates

The Medical Act 1983 provides that if a medical certificate has to be signed by virtue of any statute that means that it must be signed by a fully registered medical practitioner. Section 48 states: 'A certificate required by any enactment, whether passed before or after the commencement of this Act, from any physician, surgeon, licentiate in medicine and surgery or other medical practitioner shall not be valid unless the person signing it is fully registered'.

It must be noted that legislation relating to the National Health Service (NHS) obliges NHS practitioners to provide certain certificates free of charge.

The National Health Service Act 1977 Section 29(2)(d) and the National Health Service (Scotland) Act 1978 Section 19(2)(d) state that NHS medical practitioners must issue to patients or their personal representatives such certificates as may be prescribed if such are reasonably required by them under or for the purposes of any enactment.

In England and Wales the Terms of Service for NHS doctors as set out in the National Health Service (General Medical and Pharmaceutical Services) Regulations (S.I. 1974 No.160), as amended, provide that doctors must issue free of charge to their patients or their personal representatives the certificates listed in Schedule 3.

The list is long but includes, for example, certificates supporting claims for payment under the Social Security Act 1975, or for certain disability pensions, certificates to establish pregnancy or other medical grounds to obtain welfare foods, certificates enabling sight to be tested, certificates regarding unfitness for jury service, and certificates enabling a disabled person to be registered as an absent voter.

The doctor is excused from this obligation 'when, for the condition to which the certificate relates, the patient (a) is being attended by another doctor (other than a partner, assistant or other deputy of the first named doctor), or (b) is not being treated by, or under the supervision of, a doctor'.

In Scotland similar provisions are made in the National Health Service (General Medical and Pharmaceutical Services) (Scotland) Regulations (S.I. 1974 No.506) (S41).

9.4.1 Venereal Disease

The Venereal Diseases Act 1917 provides for the prosecution of any unqualified persons who treat venereal disease for reward. Section 1 states: '. . . a person shall not, unless he is a duly qualified medical practitioner, for reward either direct or indirect, treat any person for venereal disease or prescribe any remedy therefor, or give any advice in connection with the treatment thereof, whether the advice is given to the person to be treated or to any other person'.

9

9.4.2 Attending Maternity Cases

Section 17(1) of the Nurses, Midwives and Health Visitors Act 1979 provides: 'A person other than a registered midwife or registered medical practitioner shall not attend a woman in childbirth'.

9.5 Paramedical Professions

9.5.1 The Professions Supplementary to Medicine Act 1960

The following professions are subject to statutory control by virtue of the Professions Supplementary to Medicine Act 1960.

Chiropodists, dieticians, medical laboratory scientific officers, occupational therapists, orthoptists, physiotherapists and radiographers.

The Act set up the Council for Professions Supplementary to Medicine which co-ordinates and supervises the work of separate professional boards (also established by the Act, one for each profession).

The Council may recommend to the Privy Council that other professions be brought within the ambit of the Act or that professions currently controlled by the Act be removed from that control. The Privy Council has the power to order accordingly provided both Houses of Parliament agree that such a change should take effect.

The Boards are under a duty to promote high standards of professional education and conduct amongst members of the professions which they regulate. These duties include deciding what qualifications merit registration with the Boards, supervising training, registering those who are competent, setting professional standards and removing from the register those whose conduct merits removal.

9.5.1.1 Education and Training

Under Section 4 of the Act the Boards have the power to approve courses of training; qualifications granted after taking an examination and attending an approved course of training; and institutions as being suitable to conduct approved training courses. The Boards' approval or withdrawal of same must be sanctioned by the Privy Council before it takes effect. Under Section 5 the Boards also have a duty to supervise approved institutions and examinations for approved qualifications.

9.5.1.2 Registration

It is the duty of the Boards to maintain a register of properly qualified persons. Anyone who has attended an approved training course at an approved institution and has obtained an approved qualification is entitled to be registered following application in the prescribed manner.

9.5.1.3   Setting Professional Standards

As will be seen later, if a registered professional is judged by his disciplinary committee to be 'guilty of infamous conduct in any professional respect' that person's name can be erased from the register. The disciplinary committees of each Board are under a statutory duty to prepare and revise from time to time a statement as to the kind of conduct which they consider would amount to infamous conduct. A copy must be posted to each registered member. (Section 9(6).)

Each Board draws up its own rules but some features are common. One clause inserted in all the statements is that no practitioner should by any act or omission do anything or cause anything to be done which he has reasonable grounds for believing is likely either to endanger or to affect adversely in a substantial way the health or safety of a patient.

9.5.1.4   Discipline Under the Act

The Boards must each establish an investigating committee and a disciplinary committee. The former investigates allegations that a person's name should be removed from the register and decides whether to refer the matter to the latter, which must consider and determine any case referred to it. If a registered professional is convicted of a criminal offence which a disciplinary committee considers renders him unfit to be 'registered' or is 'judged to be guilty of infamous conduct in any professional respect' his name can be erased. Note that the fact that the conduct complained of is not specifically listed in the statement mentioned in the above paragraph does not preclude the disciplinary committee from directing erasure. The committee can also erase a name if registration was obtained by fraud and those who make false representations to obtain registration can be prosecuted in the criminal courts.

9.5.1.5   The Effect of Registration

There is no rule of law which prohibits non-registered persons from practising these professions. However, those who are registered are by virtue of Section 6 of the Act permitted to use the title 'State Registered'. Anyone who falsely pretends to be 'State Registered' when he is not can be prosecuted in the criminal courts.

By virtue of the National Health Service (Professions Supplementary to Medicine) Regulations (S.I. 1974 No.494) no member of these professions can be employed by the National Health Service (NHS) unless he is state registered. There is nothing, however, to prevent non-state registered persons being employed in the private or other sectors outside the NHS. If a licence is required though for the operation of private practice premises local authority bye-laws, for example, may restrict the grant of such licences to state registered personnel.

9.6 Indemnity Schemes

There is no general requirement that a doctor must be insured against possible negligence or other legal claims. However, some employers insist that doctors employed by them make arrangements to that effect. For example, doctors (including those doing pre-registration house jobs) who are employed to do National Health Service (NHS) work in an NHS hospital will find that their contract of employment obliges them to join a 'recognised defence organisation' or if some objection is held to joining one the doctor must 'take out and produce to the Board an insurance policy covering yourself in respect of any liability arising out of or in connection with your duties . . .'.

Other doctors such as community physicians may or may not be required to belong to a defence organisation, depending on whether or not their work has a clinical aspect.

Doctors who are not obliged to effect insurance or indemnity arrangements, eg private practitioners and general practitioners, would be foolish not to do so because apart from being liable for their own negligence they could also be held legally responsible for any negligent acts of their employees. Employers are in law 'vicariously' liable for the negligent acts of their employees regardless of rank or specialty. If a claim is made therefore against an NHS hospital doctor and that claim is successful the awarded damages may be paid jointly by the defence organisation or insurers and the health authority. The NHS has no insurance policy against such claims and is said to be 'self insuring'.

The three major defence organisations are the Medical Protection Society (MPS), the Medical Defence Union (MDU) and the Medical and Dental Defence Union of Scotland (MDDU). All three provide essentially similar services. The MDU, for example, offers the following.

'The benefits which may be granted to a member include:

1   Advice on any matter connected with a member's practice, whether in hospital, in private practice, or while serving in a public or other service.

2   Assistance in defending proceedings where a question of professional principle is involved.

3   Assistance in vindicating a member's professional interests, honour and character.

4   Assistance in proceedings brought by a patient arising from 'the act or omission of the member or of . . .'. Various persons are listed including partners, assistants, locums, subordinate medical or dental officers, assistants or subordinates who are not registered medical or dental practitioners such as nurses, dispensers etc. However, the MDU will not normally accept responsibility where the member has been engaged in activities outside the normal range of medical or dental practice.

'5 Assistance when damages and costs are awarded by a court or a settlement is made out of court.'

9.6.1 The Medical Defence Organisations and Legal Controls

It can be seen from the above that the MDU 'may' grant its members the assistance listed. If a doctor were to effect insurance with an insurance company there would be a contractual right to insist on any indemnity covered by the policy. Because of the discretionary nature of the cover offered by the MDU and the other defence bodies it was decided in the case of Medical Defence Union v Department of Trade [1979] 2 AER 421 that the medical defence organisations are not carrying on the business of insurance and are not therefore subject to the legal controls imposed upon insurance companies.

9.7 Fees charged by Doctors in NHS Hospitals

The BMA guidance note on Category 1 and 2 Work explains that a doctor employed in National Health Service (NHS) hospital work is expected to perform various categories of work in pursuance of that contract. Some examinations and reports that an NHS doctor may be required to do form part of his contractual duties and others do not. The latter, referred to as Category 2 work, may be charged for; the former, called Category 1 work, may not. The leaflet also explains that where NHS hospital facilities are used for the purposes of Category 2 work then one third of the fee payable must go to the hospital as payment for hospital costs.

If a doctor were accused of making a fraudulent claim for payment then criminal prosecution could follow. Section 15 of the Theft Act 1968 (not applicable in Northern Ireland and Scotland) provides that: 'A person who by any deception dishonestly obtains property belonging to another, with the intention of permanently depriving the other of it' can be sent to prison for up to 10 years.

'Property' includes money and cheques (Section 4(1)). When it comes to the issue of dishonesty the case of R v Ghosh [1982] QB 1053 laid down that the court must decide whether according to the ordinary standards of reasonable and honest people what was done was dishonest. If so then the court must decide whether the defendant realised his conduct was dishonest.

Section 17 of the same Act deals with the offence of false accounting defined as follows.

'(1) Where a person dishonestly, with a view to gain for himself or another or with intent to cause loss to another, -

   (a) destroys, defaces, conceals or falsifies any account or any record or document made or required for any accounting purpose; or

   (b) in furnishing information for any purpose produces or makes use of any account, or any such record or document as aforesaid, which to his

9

knowledge is or may be misleading, false or deceptive in a material particular.'

The maximum penalty is seven years in prison.

If a claim was shown to be inaccurate then a successful prosecution could follow if it could be proven beyond reasonable doubt that there was deliberate dishonesty. In other cases the money could be recovered by civil action.

In either event a doctor would risk being disciplined by the GMC. The GMC booklet lists the categories of misconduct that might lead to disciplinary proceedings under Dishonesty: Improper financial transactions (paras 52-56).

'52. A doctor is liable to disciplinary proceedings if he is convicted of criminal deception (obtaining money or goods by false pretences), forgery, fraud, theft or any other offence involving dishonesty.

53. The Council takes a particularly serious view of dishonest acts committed in the course of a doctor's professional practice (whether under the National Health Service or otherwise) or against his patients or colleagues. Such acts, if reported to the Council, may result in disciplinary proceedings. Among the circumstances which may have this result are the improper demand or acceptance of fees from patients contrary to the statutory provisions which regulate the conduct of the National Health Service and, in particular:

(a) the charging of fees to in-patients or out-patients treated at National Health Service hospitals, when the proper steps have not been taken to ensure that such patients enjoy the status of resident or non-resident private patients, as required by statute;

(b) knowingly and improperly seeking to obtain from a Family Practitioner Committee or other health authority any payment to which the doctor is not entitled, including the improper issue of National Health Service prescriptions either to patients on the doctor's dispensing list or to patients whom the doctor is treating under private contract.'

9

10 Medical Records

10.1 Ownership of Medical Records

The question of ownership of medical records is central to the vexed issue of control of information. Questions of patients' access to their medical records and control over their disclosure to third parties turn on the fact of ownership.

The concept of ownership of information is very underdeveloped in England and Wales, and at common law the person who 'controls' the records is the person who writes them. Therefore in the case of private doctors who write down the information on their writing material, they own the medical records and control what happens to them (subject of course to ethical controls on the disclosure of confidential information). Despite the fact that the information emanates from the patient telling the doctor what the matter is, and is thus in one sense the patient's, the substance of the record is an interpretation of that information as a function of the doctor's skill, and is thus his.

As regards National Health Service (NHS) records, medical records written and retained by NHS general practitioners are made on forms supplied by the Family Practitioner Committee and are expressly stated to remain their property. Similarly, medical records written by hospital doctors are made on NHS property. But as hospital doctors are employed by a health authority, any records made by them in the course of their employment are kept by the relevant health authority, and are ultimately the property of the Secretary of State.

Occupational health records of NHS staff are retained by the relevant occupational health doctor and are not made available to the employing authority automatically.

10.2 Death of Owner of Medical Records

10.2.1 England and Wales

The question of ownership of medical records has been briefly discussed above. It was pointed out that NHS records are considered to be the property of the Secretary of State. NHS hospital medical records are kept by the relevant health authorities but on the death of a NHS general practitioner, records are returned to the Family Practitioner Committee. Medical records in private cases, however, are considered to belong to the doctor, unless some agreement

10

to the contrary has been made between the doctor and patient. Consideration therefore has to be given as to what happens to the records of a private practitioner when that person dies. If the doctor has left a will then the persons named therein as the personal representatives have a duty to distribute the doctor's property in accordance with the terms of the will. If no will has been left, then property devolves upon the next of kin in accordance with a statutorily laid down order. Persons entitled to the estate can usually apply for letters of administration enabling them to administer that estate. The order is broadly speaking as follows.

1   Surviving spouse.

2   Children.

3   Parents.

4   Brothers and sisters of the whole blood, or their children if they have died already.

5   Brothers and sisters of the half blood, or their children if they have died already.

6   Grandparents.

7   Uncles and aunts of the whole blood, or their children if they have died already.

8   Uncles and aunts of the half blood, or their children if they have died already.

If the deceased had none of the above, then property devolves first on the Crown, and the Treasury may apply for letters of administration, secondly on the Duchy of Lancaster, whose solicitors may apply for letters of administration, and lastly on the Duchy of Cornwall, whose solicitors may similarly apply.

A creditor of the deceased may apply for letters of administration to administer the estate, but is not entitled to the estate itself, except to the extent of the debt owed to him.

The question is posed as to what would happen if the person entitled to ownership of the records following the death of a doctor in private practice decided to misuse them in some way, eg by selling the contents to a newspaper. The extent to which there is a legal duty of confidentiality owed to patients is discussed under Confidentiality, subchapter 2.1. It is pointed out there that private patients might well have a right to sue a doctor for damages if a breach of confidentiality occurred. It is suggested that a patient could also try to sue any person in possession of the records if they were to wrongfully disclose the contents. Once the action had been launched an immediate injunction could be applied for to restrain publication. Whether such an action would succeed is a matter for speculation. Bearing in mind the difficulties that could arise

10

doctors in private practice should be encouraged to deal with this issue in their will.

10.2.2 Scotland

In Scotland the order of succession to a moveable property in intestacy is (after the surviving spouse's prior rights have been satisfied):

1 The deceased's children and their issue.

2 Collaterals (brothers, sisters or their offspring).

3 Ascendants (parents etc).

Thereafter succession depends on whether there was or was not a surviving spouse and at the end of the day succession ends with the Crown as *ultimus haeres*.

The question of confidentiality between a private patient or the person or organisation who inherits his medical advisor's records is but one aspect of what may be a growing problem as private medical care burgeons. It is, for example, desirable that whoever takes over the care of the patient has access to the previous records and that they are not destroyed or misused by the relatives. It may be that a similar rule should be applied to private medical practitioners as applies to NHS doctors.

10.3 Recommended Length of Retention of Records

Medical records in private cases are considered to belong to the doctor unless an agreement to the contrary has been made between doctor and patient. It is therefore up to the private practitioner to decide how long he should keep those records. National Health Service (NHS) records are considered to be the property of the Secretary of State. In the case of NHS hospital records the responsibility for keeping same is vested in the relevant health authorities, to whom guidance about the issue of how long to retain them has been issued in DHSS Circular HC(80)7 (see below). A general practitioner's records are kept by the general practitioner, who returns same to the Family Practitioner Committee when the patient dies, emigrates or changes doctor.

By virtue of the Public Records Act 1958 (as amended) health authorities are under a duty to preserve such hospital records as ought to be permanently preserved and arrange for their safe keeping. Also all those who have the responsibility for keeping records need to consider, apart from the need to retain same in the interests of the patient and for research purposes, the question of retaining records in connection with possible future litigation. It is necessary in this context to consider the time limits within which legal actions can be brought.

The law on this subject is set out in the Limitation Act 1980 (England and Wales only) and in the Prescription and Limitation (Scotland) Act 1984. The

10

basic rule is that when claiming damages for personal injury or death a person must commence his legal action within three years of the action complained of (in cases where economic loss only is being claimed the time limit is six years).

Schedule 1 of the Consumer Protection Act 1987 amends both the Limitation Act 1980 and the Prescription and Limitation (Scotland) Act 1973 in respect of product liability.

A new Section 11A of the Limitation Act 1980 relating to action in respect of defective products, states:

'(1) This section shall apply to an action for damages by virtue of any provision of Part 1 of the Consumer Protection Act 1987.

(2) None of the time limits given in the preceding provisions of this Act shall apply to an action to which this section applies.'

This alters the maximum period of limitation in respect of such actions to ten years from 'the relevant time', while providing for shorter time limits similar to, but not identical with, those mentioned below.(See subchapter 3.6.5. for further details.)

A similar provision is made in the Prescription and Limitation (Scotland) Act 1973.

To the basic rule there are various exceptions as follows.

10.3.1 Subsequent knowledge

If certain criteria are met a claim in respect of personal injuries may be made within three years of the claimant discovering certain facts. In Scotland if the claimant was not aware of some material fact of a decisive nature until some date after the injury was sustained then it is possible for the claimant to bring the action within a three year period of acquiring this knowledge. In England and Wales a similar extension is allowed, ie 'three years from the date of knowledge (if later) of the person injured'. The Act spells out in some detail what the 'date of knowledge' means in this context. It means the date on which the person first had knowledge (see below) of the following facts.

1   That the injury in question was 'significant' defined as follows: '. . . if the person whose date of knowledge is in question would reasonably have considered it sufficiently serious to justify his instituting proceedings for damages against a defendant who did not dispute liability and was able to satisfy a judgement'.

2   That the injury was attributable in whole or in part to the act or omission which is alleged to constitute negligence, nuisance or breach of duty.

3   The identity of the defendant.

10

4   And, if it is alleged that the act or omission was that of a person other than the defendant, the identity of the person and the additional facts supporting the bringing of an action against the defendant.

Two further points must be borne in mind:

1   Knowledge that any acts or omissions did or did not, as a matter of law, involve negligence, nuisance or breach of duty is irrelevant.

2   A person's 'knowledge' is deemed to include '. . . knowledge which he might reasonably have been expected to acquire -

   (a) from facts observable or ascertainable by him; or

   (b) from facts ascertainable by him with the help of medical or other appropriate expert advice which it is reasonable for him to seek.'

However, if a person has taken all reasonable steps to obtain (and where appropriate act on) expert advice he shall not be deemed for these purposes to have knowledge of a fact ascertainable only with the help of expert advice.

10.3.2   Court Discretion

In addition, if given leave by the court, a claimant can be permitted to start an action outside the normal three year limit if the court considers that to give such leave would be 'equitable'. The English statute lists a number of criteria to be taken into account. The court must consider the extent to which the plaintiff would be prejudiced if the action was not allowed to proceed out of time and conversely the extent to which the defendant would be prejudiced if the court exercised discretion in favour of the plaintiff. The court must look at all the circumstances but a number of criteria are to be particularly considered:

   (a) 'the length of, and the reasons for, the delay on the part of the plaintiff;'

   (b) the extent to which, having regard to the delay, the evidence adduced by the plaintiff or the defendant is or is likely to be less cogent than if the action had been brought in time;

   (c) 'the conduct of the defendant after the cause of action arose, including the extent (if any) to which he responded to requests reasonably made by the plaintiff for information or inspection for the purpose of ascertaining facts which were or might be relevant to the plaintiff's cause of action.' (Doctors or hospitals faced with queries from dissatisfied patients should particularly note this provision and should immediately seek legal advice if appropriate.)

   (d) the duration of any disability of the plaintiff arising after the date of the accrual of the action (examples of legal 'disabilities' are mental illness or being under the age of 18);

10

131

(e) 'the extent to which the plaintiff acted promptly and reasonably once he knew whether or not the act or omission of the defendant, to which the injury was attributable, might be capable at that time of giving rise to an action for damages;'

(f) 'the steps, if any, taken by the plaintiff to obtain medical, legal or other expert advice and the nature of any such advice he may have received'.

The net result of the above is that a doctor could be sued some years after giving treatment even though a general time limit of three years applies.

There are in addition two other exceptions as follows:

1   Minors in England and Wales

A person who wishes to claim damages for a personal injury allegedly sustained whilst he was under the age of 18 has the right to commence a legal action in respect of that injury within three years of his attaining the age of 18. Such a person could also claim the benefit of the two exceptions mentioned above.

Note too, that under the Congenital Disabilities (Civil Liability) Act 1976 (not applicable in Scotland) a person may sue for injuries received whilst in the womb if these result from the negligent actions of a person other than his mother (unless injured by mother's negligent driving at a time when she knew or should reasonably have known she was pregnant). It is of interest to note that Section 1(5) provides as follows.

'The defendant is not answerable to the child, for anything he did or omitted to do when responsible in a professional capacity for treating or advising the parent, if he took reasonable care having due regard to then received professional opinion applicable to the particular class of case; but this does not mean that he is answerable only because he departed from received opinion.'

The net result of the above is that if a doctor is treating a pregnant woman it is possible that a legal action could result within 21 years of the birth. In the case of other children an action could be started within three years of their attaining the age of 18. Also if an exceptional case could be made out to the court it could be even longer.

In Scotland in terms of the 1984 Act no account is to be taken in computing the periods within which an action has to be raised or any time during which the injured person was under a legal disability by reason of nonage [ie a minor or pupil] or unsoundness of mind. In addition the provisos relating to the date of knowledge and to the Court's discretion can be invoked.

10

2 Mentally Ill Persons

In England and Wales a person who allegedly suffered personal injuries at a time when he was of unsound mind may sue for damages within three years of recovering his sanity. A person of 'unsound mind' is someone who by reason of mental disorder as defined in the Mental Health Act 1983 is incapable of managing or administering his property and affairs. Such incapacity is assumed if the patient is being compulsorily detained or is subject to guardianship under the Act or if following such detention or guardianship the patient is continuing to receive voluntary in-patient treatment.

10.3.3 *Retention of records by NHS Hospitals*

Bearing in mind the above, the DHSS Circular already referred to (HC(80)7) recommends to NHS hospitals minimum periods for which records should be retained as follows:

(a) Obstetric records: 25 years.

(b) Records relating to children and young people (including paediatric, vaccination and community child health service records): until the patient's 25th birthday or eight years after the last entry if longer.

(c) Records relating to mentally disordered persons within the meaning of the Mental Health Act: 20 years from the date at which, in the opinion of the doctor concerned, the disorder has ceased or diminished to the point where no further care or treatment is considered necessary.

(Except that such records need only be retained for a minimum of eight years after the death of a patient, or in the case of obstetric records, death of the child – but not of the mother.)

(d) All other personal health records: eight years after the conclusion of the treatment.

As records could be required in litigation virtually without limit of time the Department recognises that inevitably records might be destroyed which subsequently are wanted for litigation. They state that if this happens any prejudice thereby occasioned should be taken into account if damages are later apportioned between the doctor and the health authority.

10.4 Data Protection Act 1984

The Data Protection Act, which received Royal Assent in July 1984, protects individuals from the misuse of personal information recorded in a form in which it can be processed by equipment operating automatically in response to instructions given for that purpose, eg held on a computer. Anyone who controls the content and use of personal data is required to register under the Act.

As from 11 May 1986 data subjects have been entitled to compensation from data users if it can be proved that they have suffered damage because of:

10

1   loss of personal data
2   unauthorised destruction of personal data
3   unauthorised disclosure of personal data
4   inaccurate personal data

As from 11 November 1987 data subjects have had the right to have access to information about them contained in data.

10.4.1   Data Protection Principles

The principles as set out in Schedule 1 of the Data Protection Act are:

The First Principle – 'The information to be contained in personal data shall be obtained and personal data shall be processed, fairly and lawfully.'

The Second Principle – 'Personal data should be held only for one or more specified and lawful purposes.'

The Third Principle – 'Personal data held for any purpose or purposes shall not be used to disclose in any manner incompatible with that purpose or those purposes.'

The Fourth Principle – 'Personal data held for any purpose or purposes shall be adequate, relevant and not excessive in relation to that purpose or those purposes.'

The Fifth Principle – 'Personal data shall be accurate and, where necessary, kept up to date.'

The Sixth Principle – 'Personal data held for any purpose or purposes shall not be kept for longer than is necessary for that purpose or those purposes.'

The Seventh Principle – 'An individual shall be entitled -

(a)   at reasonable intervals and without undue delay or expense -

i   to be informed by any Data User whether he holds personal data of which that individual is the subject; and

ii   to access to any such data held by a Data User; and

(b)   where appropriate, to have such data corrected or erased.'

The Eighth Principle – 'Appropriate security measures shall be taken against unauthorised access to, or alteration, disclosure or destruction of, personal data and against loss or destruction of personal data.'

10.4.2   Registrar's Duties

The Data Protection Registrar's duties include the maintenance of a register of data users who hold personal data and of providers of bureau computer services to persons in control of personal data. He has the power to execute legal penalties against individuals in regard to a wide variety of offences connected with the Act. This includes the power to initiate legal action against any person holding or using data not covered by their registration entry, or in a manner not consistent with that entry or with the 'Data Protection Principles'.

10.4.3 Subject Access Modification (Health) Order

As stated above, the provisions of the Data Protection Act relating to subject access came into effect on 11 November 1987 and consequently gave patients the right of access to all personal information held on them by doctors and other health professionals (ie data users). The Data Protection Act (Subject Access Modification) (Health) Order 1987 was issued subsequently by the Home Secretary.

This Order allows a doctor who believes that serious harm will result to the physical or mental health of a patient if full access were provided to erase harmful data. However, no definition is given as to what constitutes serious harm.

10.4.4 General practitioners

The BMA's General Medical Services Committee has prepared guidance in the form of two booklets for general practitioners who need to register under the Data Protection Act. The first on subject access provisions was published in December 1987, and the second on registration in March 1988.

10.4.5 Health authorities

Guidance to health authorities on modified access to personal health information was issued in Health Circular HC(87)14 in September 1987 prior to the issue of the Order (see above). A further Health Circular HC(87)25 (HC(FP)(89)9) issued in November 1987 gives advice as to the rights of children and parents under the Act.

10